THE EDDIE BAUER OUTDOOR LIBRARY

Eddie Bauer, Inc., has been serving the needs of outdoor enthusiasts for three generations. Since 1920, we have been dedicated to developing, testing, and manufacturing the finest in apparel and gear for outdoor adventures. Our aim has been to make outdoor adventures more enjoyable.

Now, over sixty-five years later, Eddie Bauer is answering the needs of another generation of outdoor activists. Eddie Bauer Outdoor Guides like this one on Fly Fishing will help newcomers get started. All of the guides contain up-to-date, tested information to make your outdoor excursions safe, warm, dry, and comfortable.

CONTENTS

Flyfishing

PART I
THE ANGLER'S WORLD

CHAPTER 1

WHY FLY FISHING?

"In angling, fly fishing has a special hold on the spirit of man. This is because, of all forms, it requires a perfect balance between discipline and freedom."

— *Anon.*

The singular appeal of fly fishing has been the subject of an enormous amount of writing. And, oddly, this body of material is about equally divided between poetic rhapsody and extremely technical detail. It is difficult to think of another sport in

1

which precision technique and specialized knowledge are so balanced with philosophy.

To the non-fly fisherman this compound of the poetic and the technical has often seemed elitist, too purist, too "mystical." The point of fishing, after all, is to catch fish, and what does it matter how you catch them?

But to the fly fisherman, this misses the point entirely. He certainly wants to catch fish, and devotes an extraordinary amount of ingenuity, time, and energy to that end. But it is not, after all, the *only* point.

The fly fisherman is not only interested in the final product, he is interested, if that is the word, in the activity itself. It is the *act* of fishing from which he derives his pleasure, not just the end result. It is the enchantment of the game that occupies his attention, not the score.

Someone once defined the perfect game as one that had only one rule, and for which the possibilities of combination were infinite.

FLY FISHING

Angling with an artificial bait: a fish hook dressed with hair, feathers, thread, tinsel, etc., so as to resemble an insect or small fish.

Fly fishing comes as close, perhaps, to that perfect game as any other activity we know. It can be played by the complete novice with great satisfaction, but there is no end to the refining of his skills.

What is there about fly fishing that is so enticing? What makes it different from any other form of angling?

The major physical difference seems quite trivial, but it may be the key to why the pleasure of fly fishing is different from other techniques.

In other forms of casting, the angler is throwing a weight on the end of a line, whether it be a lure or a sinker. It certainly requires great precision, but it is essentially like heaving a rock in the water.

The fly fisherman is casting with only the weight of the line itself, a weight distributed over 30 or 40 feet. The tiny fly at the line's end is almost weightless and provides no momentum at all.

Whereas many sports require strength, fly fishing requires delicacy, a fine touch. To control that length of line floating in the air is probably what our anonymous author meant by a balance between discipline and freedom.

This is probably why fly fishing has been the preferred technique of so many skilled women. In fact, the first complete text on fly fishing was written by a woman, 150 years before Izaak Walton ever wafted a stonefly over the glorious Lea.

In 1496, while Columbus was still trying to persuade Europe there was something valuable over here, Dame Juliana Berners published "A Treatyse of Fysshynge with an Angle." In it she described twelve styles of fly, with complete instructions on tying them. A century and a half later, Izaak Walton was still using the exact same patterns. Modern fishermen who have used them claim they are just as effective now as they were half a millennium ago.

The canny lady was also one of the first conservationists. She hid her treatise in the great *Boke of St. Albans*, to discourage the interest of idlers in the sport of fishing, "which they might destroy utterly by virtue of the skill acquired from this treatise."

Dame Juliana occupies a unique position as the first major authority on the sport. We will meet her again in Chapter Two, when we look briefly at the history of fly fishing.

The great naturalist John Burroughs, himself an avid fly fisherman (who claimed there were trout streams gurgling around the roots of his family tree), also suggests another aspect of difference between fly fishing and other techniques.

> I have been a seeker of trout since boyhood, and on all expeditions in which this fish has been the ostensible purpose I have brought home more than my creel showed. I find I got more of nature into me, more of the woods, the wild, nearer to bird and beast, while threading streams for trout than in any other way. It furnished a good excuse to go forth; it pitched one in the right key.

This harmony with nature is probably the most common theme in the poetic visions of the fly fishermen-authors of the past. It has not always been a popular view, particularly in those periods when our main interest seems to have been the domination of nature for profit.

In recent decades, of course, we have revitalized the notion of man in harmony with his surroundings, and it is not surprising to find that fly fishermen have been among the leaders in movements to protect the integrity of natural places.

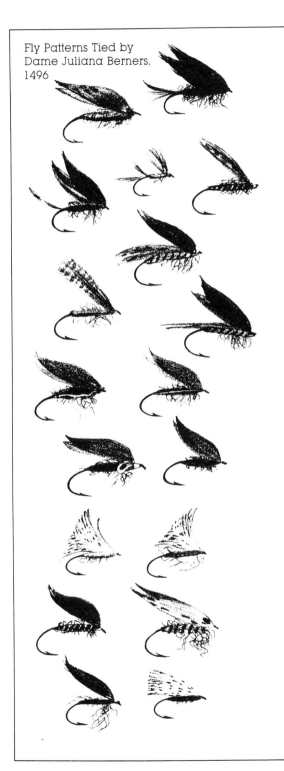

Fly Patterns Tied by Dame Juliana Berners, 1496

And more than simply espousing a cause verbally, they have, as a group, let their actions reflect what they believe. It is rare indeed to find a fly fisherman who keeps more fish than he needs. And in fact, the majority probably now fish with barbless hooks, so their catch can be released unharmed. Once again, the pleasure is in the process, not the product.

The image of the trout fisherman on a mountain stream is probably the most common one associated with fly fishing. But it is much more limited than the sport itself.

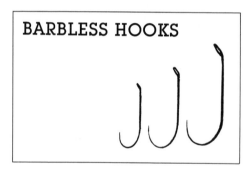

BARBLESS HOOKS

Fly fishing is not by any means restricted to trout, nor is it restricted to fresh water. It has even been suggested that the reason so much has been written about trout is that trout fishermen will pay money for books and bass fishermen won't.

Remember that fly fishing is primarily a technique of fishing in general, and that it long precedes spin casting and artificial lures and plastic worms. Practically every fish that can be taken has been taken on an artificial fly.

There are certainly enough different varieties of fly pattern to accommodate the fisherman, no matter whether his home ground is streams, or rivers, or lakes, or saltwater.

Artificial flies are categorized according to what they imitate:
1. The dry fly imitates a flying insect that has landed on the surface of the water.
2. The wet fly imitates an insect that has fallen into the water, and begun to sink.
3. The nymph imitates the earlier, larval stage of an insect born in the water.
4. Streamers and bucktails imitate small baitfish.
5. Terrestrials imitate land insects that have fallen in the water and drowned.

From this you can see that an extremely wide range of fish can be tempted with the artificial fly. No matter where you are, or what your local favorite catch is, there will be plenty of fly fishing opportunity.

The anonymous writer quoted above also says:

> No tool ever invented by man is so sensitive to his intentions as a good fly rod. Like courting a beautiful woman, a delicate touch is required. We entice, we cajole, we persuade and, yes, we deceive. Our art is an art of illusion in the end. And it is not merely a brainless fish that we deceive, but the millions of years of Mother Nature's intuition. That is no small accomplishment, my friend.

The novice is sometimes intimidated by the mystique that surrounds the sport, and the immense body of technical information on methods of casting, reading of waters, types of fly, and the endless anecdotes about this or that perfect cast. He gets the impression that he will have to spend a year in study or he will appear a fool at streamside.

This, of course, is nonsense. With a few hours of practice, almost anyone can learn enough of the technique to have the pleasures of the sport at his disposal.

The main purpose of this book is to provide you with the basic information that will get you started—and enjoying yourself—as quickly as possible. And secondarily, to point out the directions in which your skills can be refined. We will provide the basic information, and beyond that, your own experience will teach you more than any book can.

CHAPTER 2

A BIT OF ANGLING HISTORY

In undertaking to go fly fishing, you stand in a stream of history that goes back more than two thousand years. If you tie your own flies—a delightful, as well as useful, hobby—you will tie them much as the Macedonian fisherman of 200 B.C. tied his.

At the same time, you will be using high-technology products that were not even dreamed of until the space race.

The first written reference of fly fishing comes from the Roman poet Martial who wrote:

Who has not seen the scarus rise
Decoyed and killed by false flies.

A couple of hundred years later
there came a long passage from another Roman, Aelian. This is worth
quoting at length, because it dem-
onstrates the sophistication fly fishing
had already acquired. Except that it
is a translation from Latin, it would be
difficult to distinguish from a description written today. The fish itself even
appears to be a Macedonian trout.

I have heard of a Macedo-
nian way of catching fish: between Beroea and Thessalonica
runs a river called the Astraeus,
and in it there are fish with speckled skins. What they are called,
you had best ask the Macedo-
nians.

These fish feed on a fly peculiar to the country, which hov-
ers on the river. It is not like flies
found elsewhere, nor does it resemble a wasp in appearance.

Nor would one describe it as a
midge or bee, yet it has something of each of these.

In boldness it is like a fly, in
size you might call it a midge. It
imitates the color of a wasp, and
it hums like a bee. The natives
generally call it Hippouros.

These flies seek their food
over the river, but do not escape
the observation of the fish swimming below. When the fish ob-
serves a fly on the surface, it
swims quietly up, afraid to stir
the water above, lest it should
scare away its prey.

Then, coming up by its
shadow, it opens its mouth gently
and gulps down the fly, like a
wolf carrying off a sheep from
the fold, or an eagle a goose
from the farmyard; having done
this, it goes below the rippling
water.

Now, though the fishermen
know of this, they do not use

BEGINNER'S OUTFIT

Rod: 8 to 8½ foot Fiberglas rod, weighing 3½ to 3¾ ounces, with a medium action.

Line: 6 or 7 weight.

Reel: single action

The first priority in putting together your outfit is the weight of line. Once you've chosen the proper line for your kind of fishing, selection of the rod will come about almost automatically.

The American Fishing Tackle Manufacturers Association numbers lines from 1 to 15. The most common sizes are classified by the following standard:

AFTMA FLY LINE STANDARDS

Line number	Weight in grains
1	60
2	80
3	100
4	120
5	140
6	160
7	185
8	210
9	240
10	280
11	330
12	380

these flies at all for bait; for if a man's hand touch them, they lose their natural color, their wings wither, and they become unfit food for the fish.

But the fishermen have planned a snare for the fish, and get the better of them by their fisherman's craft.

They fasten red wool around a hook, and fix on to the wool two feathers of a waxy color, which grow under a cock's wattles. Their rod is six feet long, and their line is the same length.

Then they throw their snare, and the fish, attracted and maddened by the color, comes straight at it, thinking from the pretty sight to get a dainty mouthful. When, however, it opens its jaws, it is caught by the hook and enjoys a bitter meal, a captive.

There, in a nutshell, are the principles of fishing with an artificial fly, set down fully almost two thousand years ago.

Between the Macedonian trout and Dame Juliana Berners there lie a thousand years and a thousand miles. But then, what is a millennium more or less to a fly fisherman?

Dame Juliana was then Prioress of Sopwell, England. Her treatise was included in a new edition of *The Boke of St. Albans*, which had originally been published some ten years earlier. The book was a kind of reference work for the training of young gentlemen, dealing with falconry, heraldry, and hunting.

Dame Juliana, in addition to having a clear mastery of her sport, was also astonishingly modern in her outlook. Her comments would not sound out of place in any current treatise on fishing behavior. She is also the first person to deal with what might be called the "ethics" of fly fishing. Remember that she is giving this advice in 1496:

> I charge you, that you break no man's hedges in going about your sports, nor open any man's gates without shutting them again. Also, you must not use this aforesaid artful sport for covetousness, merely for the increasing or saving of your money, but mainly for your enjoyment and to procure the health of your body, and more especially, of your soul.

Incidentally, much of the benefit to the soul seen by this extraordinary woman was that fly fishing circumvented the vice of Idleness—"which is the principal cause inciting a man to many other vices, as is right well known."

So if you are accused of merely wasting time in your new sport, you may refer your critics to the ultimate authority, Dame Juliana Berners.

In addition to her concern with the angler's soul, Dame Juliana was also a stern proponent of what we would now call "environmentalism."

> Also, you must not be too greedy in catching your said game, as in taking too much at one time, a thing which can easily happen if you do in every point as this present treatise shows you. That could easily be the occasion of destroying your own sport and other men's also.
> When you have a sufficient

mess, you should covet no more at that time. Also you should busy yourself to nourish the game in everything that you can, and to destroy all such things as are devourers of it.

> And all those that do according to this rule will have the blessing of God and St. Peter.

Through her treatise, we also have a complete picture of the fly fishing technology of her time. This is what the well-outfitted fly fisherman would be using, circa A.D. 1500.

His rod was long, up to 18 feet, and very limber. It was a sophisticated construction, evenly tapered from butt to tip. Butt, middle section, and tip were sometimes made of different woods, according to their characteristics of flexibility. The butt might be made of aspen or willow, the middle section of green hazel, and the tip of crabtree or juniper.

A fly rod made of these woods and carefully tapered would have very similar characteristics to our modern rods.

Line, however, was a different matter. You will remember that our Macedonian fishermen used a line of approximately the same length as his rod, 6 feet. Short line (by our standards) was still the rule in Dame Juliana's day. Even later, the recommendation was for a line no longer than the rod itself, and tied to the tip.

There was, of course, very good reason for this. The lines were hand-braided strands of horsehair:

> First you must take, from the tail of a white horse, the longest and best hair that you can find, and the rounder it is, the better

it is. Divide it into six bunches, and you must color every part by itself in a different color, such as yellow, green, brown, tawny, russet and dusky colors.

Dame Juliana is here giving the directions for preparing a camouflaged line! She even recommends the specific dyes to match a certain color of water or growth.

With her instructions on fly patterns, we are once again in the "modern" era.

She details a dozen patterns, and categorizes them by the month of the year in which the flies are commonly found. Some of her patterns are still used today, almost without change. And in them the modern fly fisherman certainly finds the origin of such currently popular patterns as the Black Gnat, the Wooly Worm, the Stonefly, March Brown, Whirling Dun, and Alder.

was the appearance of Izaak Walton's *Compleat Angler* in 1653.

For more than three hundred years, Izaak Walton has been seen as the patron saint of angling, and of fly fishing in particular. Oddly enough, it was not Walton, but his friend Charles Cotton, who contributed the material on fly fishing to the *Compleat Angler*. Walton himself mostly fished, and wrote about fishing, with bait.

The fly fishing portion of *The Compleat Angler* did not even appear until the fifth edition, some quarter of a century after first publication. But it was a bombshell.

It is difficult to imagine the popularity of *The Compleat Angler*. At one time in its history it was outsold only by the Bible and *Pilgrim's Progress*.

The flies described by Cotton very closely resemble those of Dame Juliana. His rod was somewhere around 16 to 18 feet long, and his line perhaps 6 feet longer.

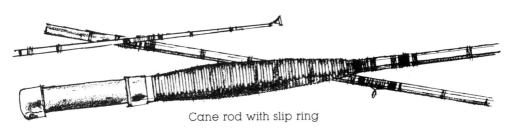

Cane rod with slip ring

Some years ago Al McClane of *Field and Stream* commissioned the expert Helen Shaw to replicate Dame Juliana's patterns in the materials and techniques of the time. The results are reproduced in color in his 1953 book *The Practical Fly Fisherman*.

In the century that followed Dame Juliana's "Treatyse" there were a number of minor works that touched on fly fishing, but the next major event

The line was still laid of horsehair, but Cotton describes for the first time the use of a tapered line. And what a job it was to create a tapered line of horsehair!

The end of the line, nearest the fly, consisted of two single hairs, about as fragile a line as one can imagine. An additional hair was added to each section as the line approached the rod, until the thickest part consisted of

Charles Cotton's fishing house on the Dove River

seven hairs laid together. "By which means," Cotton writes:

> your rod and tackle will in a manner be tapered from your very hand to your hook, your line will fall much better and straighten and cast your fly to any certain place to which the hand and eye shall direct it, with less weight and violence than would otherwise circle the water, and fright away the fish.

The two-hair strand, corresponding to what we now call the tippet, was perhaps not as precarious as it sounds. It has been estimated in modern times that the breaking strength would have averaged about 5 pounds, somewhere in the middle of the range used by today's fishermen.

In the early 1800s, linemakers began mixing silk with the braided horsehair, and this development eventually spelled the end of horsehair lines, though they were still occasionally sold in England up to World War II. By the time of the Civil War, the first all-silk lines had appeared, treated with an oily coating to make them water resistant.

Silk lines were the standard for almost a century, and they are perhaps the only piece of fishing gear poetically mentioned as part of a romantic seduction. Remember John Donne's famous poem?

But it is clear that, in fly fishing, the line was still tied to the end of the pole in his time.

By 1800, however, reels were in common use in a wide variety of styles, and that probably includes fly fishing.

In the traditional form of the fly fisherman's art, the reel is less important than in other kinds of fishing. It is primarily a place to store line, and

---

Come live with me, and be my love,
And we will some new pleasures prove
Of golden sands, and crystal brooks,
With silken lines, and silver hooks.

The first nylon line appeared in 1948, and from that point onward the synthetic materials have totally dominated the field. In 1952, a technological breakthrough permitted making an automatically tapered line with extreme precision. We are a long way from our two horsehairs.

The history of reels is not so well documented. Izaak Walton speaks of a "wheele" used by some, "about the middle of their rod, or near the hand."

doesn't play a significant role in casting or fighting the fish as it does elsewhere. The modern single-action reel is a much simpler device than a spinning reel, or even a bait-casting reel.

The fly rod, however, has always been the primary tool. It is the fisherman's entire connection with the world in which he plays, and has doubtless been given more ingenious thought than any other instrument he uses, except the fly itself.

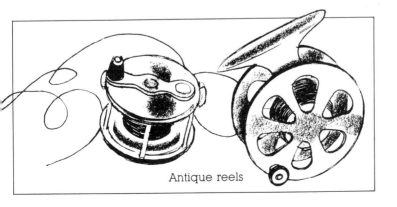

Antique reels

In Dame Juliana's day (and Izaak Walton's as well), the rod was very much longer than it is now. This was partly due to the fact that casting great lengths of line was unknown; the fly was simply presented from the end of the pole with relatively short line. But the 18-foot rod, made of carefully balanced woods, was even then a highly sensitive instrument. The woods recommended by Dame Juliana reveal a very sophisticated understanding of the "action" of a rod.

The cane rod, made of bamboo, was an extraordinarily precise creation, requiring such a degree of skill from its makers that the great ones became almost legendary.

As with line, the cane rod evolved more or less gradually from the solid woods. And this development, which was to change rod-making forever, occurred in America.

As far as we can determine, it was a Pennsylvania rod-maker, Samuel Phillipi, who created the first bamboo rod in 1845. The butt itself was of ash, but the second joint and tip were made of three splits of bamboo.

Fifteen years later, a New Jersey rod-maker produced the first all-bamboo rod. It was made of four splits, and had a roughly square cross-section.

The cane rod is not a simple bamboo pole; it is an extremely sophisticated construction of strips of bamboo glued together.

The inner part of bamboo is soft and pithy, and was never used in rod-making. Rather, it was the tough "skin" of the bamboo, and part of the hard inner core just beneath, that was used.

Long strips of the supple reed were planed to fit together perfectly over the entire length of the rod, and then glued together. Over the years, many different configurations were tried, ranging from two to twelve strips.

All this experimentation was necessary because of the demands placed on a fly rod. Not only must it be simultaneously strong and flexible, but it must bend equally well in *any* direction.

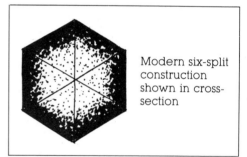

Modern six-split construction shown in cross-section

In time, the hexagonal cross-section, made with six splits, became the standard of the trade, offering the best combination of properties. By the turn of the century, most rod-makers were using the six-split method.

Again, it was the introduction of the synthetic materials, in this case Fiberglas, that changed everything.

The first Fiberglas rod appeared in the early 1950s, and it was immediately recognized that eventually the synthetic materials would replace the natural cane. Modern manufacturing techniques make superb rods available at a reasonable cost, and probably have much to do with the explosive growth of fly fishing after World War II.

There is, of course, a great deal

of nostalgia about the glories of the handmade bamboo rod. There are certainly still fishermen who claim the synthetic rod will never have the perfection of a finely crafted bamboo rod.

These men will be somewhat rueful at seeing a discussion of cane rods in a chapter on the *history* of fly fishing; but history it is. The chances are thousands to one that you will be fishing with a rod of Fiberglas, or graphite, or boron.

And although you will be practicing a skill that is thousands of years old (and has changed in principle very little), none of the tackle you use was possible until about thirty years ago.

Fly fishing today is a wonderful amalgam of deep history and modern high-tech. And, if your nostalgia for the past becomes too great, you can always braid your tippet of two horsehairs.

It is, at least, guaranteed to increase your appreciation of monofilament nylon.

Flyfishing

PART II

GETTING READY

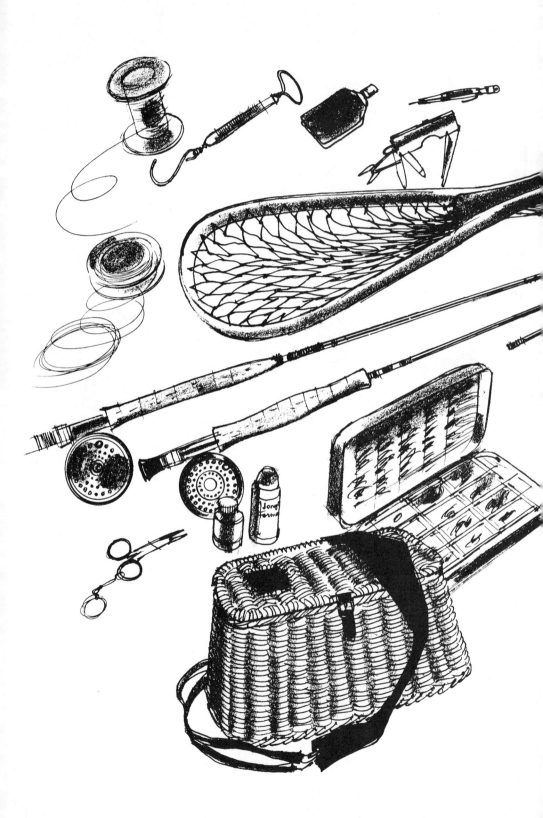

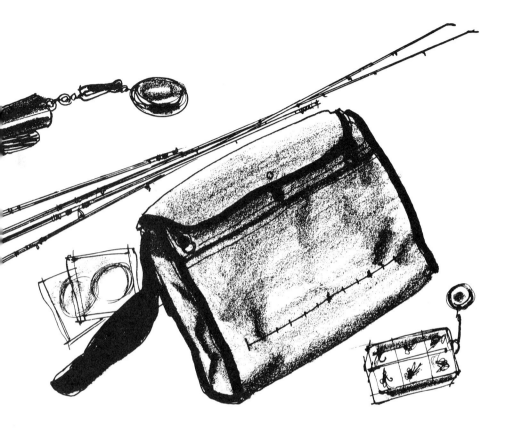

CHAPTER 3

GEAR AND TACKLE

The literature of fly fishing tackle is enormous and detailed. Fortunately, the choice of your first equipment is comparatively simple.

THE FLY ROD

The closest thing to an all-purpose fly rod is probably an 8- to 8½-foot Fiberglas rod, weighing 3½ to 3¾ ounces, with a medium action.

Such a rod will not be very far off from the kind of fishing you do, although as you become more experienced you may want to add more specialized rods for lighter or heavier fishing, or for special conditions.

Fly rods are currently made of bamboo, Fiberglas, graphite, and the latest high-tech material, boron. Boron is often found in a boron/graphite combination.

Fiberglas is by far the most economical, and it is often possible to find a perfectly adequate first rod for something under $50.

A good bamboo rod can easily cost ten times as much as Fiberglas, as can the new boron rods. Graphite is somewhere in between.

There is no question that a graphite rod is a better and more sophisti-

---

ANGLER'S HINT

Put a light coating of Armour All on your fly line to make it shoot better and increase casting distance.

---

cated casting tool than Fiberglas. These newer rods will improve almost anyone's casting, and in some respects are even more important for the beginner. (It's often said that an expert would automatically cast well with a broomstick.) As your interest in the sport progresses, you should certainly think about moving to graphite or boron.

However, for the beginner who is operating on a limited budget, Fiberglas offers the best compromise between price and performance.

Perhaps the most important thing in putting together your first kit is to be certain that the rod and line are well matched. Modern fly rods are

generally marked as to the matching line, with a designation like "5 or 6," indicating the appropriate line weight for that rod.

The size rod you choose, incidentally, will be determined by the line weight you wish to use. That is, you will make a decision about line weight *before* you make your decision about the rod.

The 6 weight line is, in a sense, a dividing point in line weights. Lines lighter than this would be favored if most of your fishing were done on smooth-surfaced, small streams, where a delicate presentation of the fly was the paramount consideration.

Lines of weight 6 and heavier are good for more turbulent waters and longer distances, where you are probably casting "blind," and using more wind-resistant flies like bucktails or streamers.

In short, the trade-off is between delicacy and power.

Your tackle shop will be able to provide more specific advice for your area. Generally speaking, you will find that the outfitters in your region will be the most knowledgeable source of information on local conditions. And you may rest assured of getting lots of advice from other anglers you encounter.

Fly rods are classified by length, weight, and action. In recent years they have also been matched with a specific line weight.

Length and weight are convenient measurements, but in fact they don't tell you as much about the character of the rod as do the action and the line recommendations.

The critical factor in the design of a rod is the way it transfers the energy

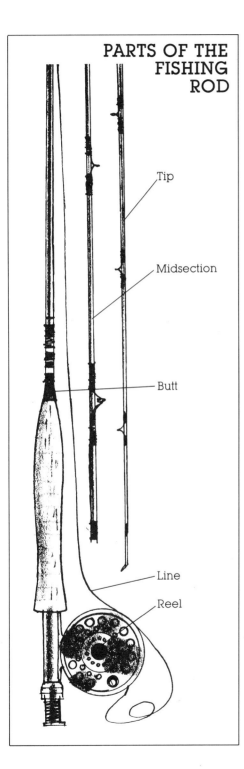

PARTS OF THE FISHING ROD

Tip

Midsection

Butt

Line

Reel

of the fisherman's arm to the fly itself. It is not as simple a matter as it may first appear.

A rod consists of four easily discernible sections: the butt, the middle section, the tip, and the line.

Now, while the line is not normally considered a *part* of the rod, in physical fact it is exactly that. The instant that force is exerted, the entire system of rod, line, and fly becomes a single, dynamic entity that must be considered as a whole.

The force of the fisherman's cast is transmitted to the butt, the butt drives the midsection, the midsection drives the tip, and the tip drives the line.

This system of linkages is what determines the action of a fly rod, and whether the power will be smoothly transmitted from beginning to end. Each of these parts must be perfectly in harmony with the others, not too stiff or too flexible, not too tight or too loose.

The "action" of a rod was traditionally classified as:

1. wet-fly action
2. dry-fly action
3. bass-steelhead action
4. salmon action

These are listed in increasing order of stiffness. This traditional classification is giving way to a simpler, three point scale of

1. slow
2. medium
3. fast

In some ways the older classification is more informative, so we have included it for your reference.

The "softest" rod is the wet-fly action. The logic here is that very little false casting is done in wet-fly fishing, so that the slight extra stiffness of the dry-fly action is unnecessary.

This does not mean that you cannot use a high-quality wet-fly action for dry-fly fishing, or vice-versa. The categories overlap a good deal, and it is not worth your while to become

your casting distance rarely exceeds 40 feet.

The rod should have a comparatively slow casting cycle, so that it can hold 20 to 40 feet of line in the air without requiring excessive speed. The small stream is a stream for del-

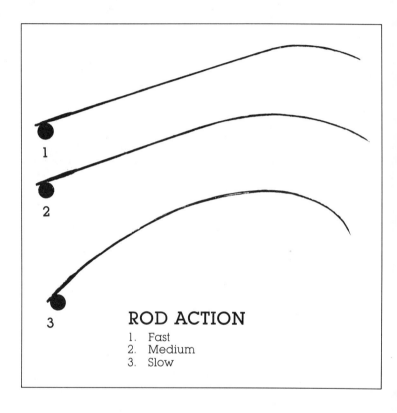

ROD ACTION
1. Fast
2. Medium
3. Slow

bogged down in details at the beginning. However, for the time when you wish to match your rod more perfectly to your fishing conditions, here are a few guidelines.

SMALL STREAMS
The most important quality in a rod for small streams is its ability to handle the lighter range of lines. Many experts feel that a DT-4-F is about ideal for fishing shallow, clear water, where

icacy and precision. Power and distance are secondary.

LARGE STREAMS
The case is different for the fisherman who is waist deep in a windswept river, casting a bushy dry fly or a bucktail to 50 or 60 foot range.

He needs to put more power into his cast, and in turbulent water the disturbance of a heavier line will scarcely matter. The large stream fisherman will want a rod to handle a 6 or 7 weight line and up. He may, in fact, use a weight-forward line (see Fly Lines) for greater distance. His rod should be more powerful, capable of

wind. A real bomber may be 9 to 10 feet long and weigh 3 to 7 ounces, depending on material. A rod of this size will have enormous casting power, but it may be a wrist-breaker

TWO MODERN FLY REELS

(left) Single-action
(right) Automatic

throwing 60 to 70 feet of line in a normal wind.

THE HEAVY RODS

For steelhead and bonefish, bass and salmon, we get into the heavy artillery of fly rods. Weight-forward lines of 8 to 12 are most common, requiring a rod with some real belt behind it.

The rod for this kind of fishing should have the power to shoot a long distance with a single back cast, and to propel large flies even against the

over a number of hours of steady casting.

In saltwater fly fishing, a rapidly growing category of the sport, even heavier line is used. For tarpon, bonefish, and even sailfish, rods capable of handling 10 to 12 weight line are used.

FLY REELS

The primary purpose of a reel is to store extra line. Some types, by means of adjustable line tension, also assist in fighting the hooked fish.

In fly fishing, reels play a somewhat less important role than in some other kinds of fishing. Your choice of reel will probably have very little to do with how many fish you catch. Here as in everything else, however, a well-made, high-quality tool will be more pleasurable to work with.

Fly fishing reels are of two kinds, single-action and automatic. Manufacturers make both these types in a wide variety of prices and qualities, and it will be very easy to find something to your taste at a comparatively reasonable price.

The single-action reel is so called because a single rotation of the handle produces a single rotation of the drum. Many good fly fishing reels have no drag mechanism built in at all, only enough to prevent the reel from overrunning. In older reels, drag is provided by the fisherman's finger pressure on the rotating spool. Modern reels, however, are most often made with exposed rims, and the angler exerts pressure by "palming" the rim itself.

The exception to this is found in reels specifically designed for saltwater fishing. These reels, which sometimes carry up to 400 yards of backing, have highly sophisticated drag mechanisms for fighting the larger saltwater species.

The automatic reel has a small lever conveniently placed, which, when depressed, automatically reels in slack line. This can be a much speedier way of getting up tight to a fish, and for this reason is a favorite with some anglers.

The primary disadvantage of the automatic reel is its smaller line capacity. It cannot hold both your fly line and any substantial amount of

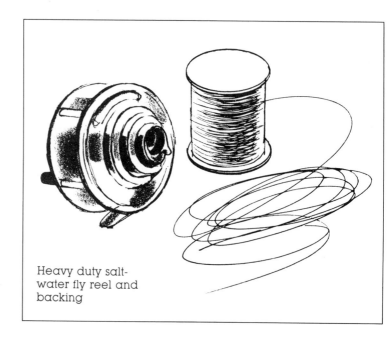

Heavy duty salt-
water fly reel and
backing

backing. If you hook a fish that makes a long run, you run the risk of coming abruptly to the end of the automatic reel's capacity. The chances are good that if he is still running when the line is fully extended, he will break your tippet and be off.

Generally speaking, the automatic reel has no substantial advantage over the single action, and in addition is heavier and more complicated. We recommend the ordinary single-action reel for all uses.

FLY LINES

From the discussion of rods above, it is clear that the main factor in your kit is the line itself; the rod is ultimately chosen because it suits the proper line for your particular fishing. Every combination of rod and line is a law unto itself. A happily matched pair will bring you hours of enjoyment, while a mismatch is an endless frustration.

Before getting into the specifics of type and weight, let's consider the qualities a fly line must have to perform well.

The fly itself is nearly weightless, so the line must provide the casting weight. In any form of casting, performance is hindered greatly when the cast lure is either too heavy or too light. The same is true in a fly rod if the *line* weight is too heavy or too light.

Too light a line will not have sufficient weight to "load" the rod—that is, put tension on it—in order to bring out the maximum power. Too heavy a line will overload the rod, reducing its ability to straighten and propel the line properly.

A well-designed line (when properly cast) will not sag in the air. It will turn over smoothly, and keep its weight off the water until the cast is completed and the fly gently deposited on the surface.

In order to do that, the weight of the line must be distributed over a shape that will maintain its velocity against the resistance of the air for the longest time possible.

Fly lines are made in different weights. The classification is determined by the weight of the first 30 feet of line, the portion that is performing the work during a cast.

The American Fishing Tackle Manufacturers Association (AFTMA), which numbers lines from 1 to 15, provides standards (see p. 9) for the most common sizes.

Rod manufacturers mark the recommended line weight directly on the rod (e.g., 5 or 6), and it is important to match the rod with the proper line weight to obtain the maximum performance.

In addition to weight alone, fly lines are also classified by their shape, and their floating characteristics. The complete description of a line is contained in a three-element code, such as DT-6-F, which refers to a Double Taper Line of weight 6, which Floats. The following information will allow you to decode the various line descriptions.

The first element of the code refers to shape, or line "profile." There are three main categories.

1. Level (L)
2. Double Taper (DT)
3. Weight Forward (WF) (also called torpedo taper)

LINE PROFILES

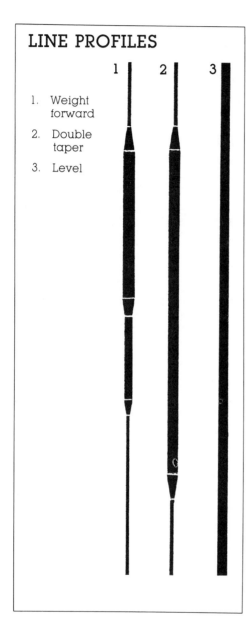

1. Weight forward
2. Double taper
3. Level

LEVEL LINE

Level line has an equal diameter throughout, and is not recommended for delicate presentations or long casts. Its only advantage is economy. It does not perform as well in any situation as the tapered profiles.

DOUBLE TAPER LINE

Double Taper has a level center and is tapered on both ends. This is currently the best-selling fly fishing taper on the market. It presents the fly more delicately than level line, and is good for spooky fish, where a minimum of water disturbance is essential.

An often-cited advantage of Double Taper line is that it can be reversed on the reel when one end becomes worn. Strictly speaking, this is true, but probably not one out of five anglers ever actually does it.

Synthetic lines have "memory." When a line has been tightly coiled around a spool for a year, it is virtually impossible to get the coils *out* of it. In order to take advantage of Double Taper's reversible qualities, you would have to switch ends every few months. Most anglers simply don't do it.

WEIGHT FORWARD LINE

The Weight Forward line, as the name implies, places most of the weight in a torpedo shape toward the tip end. It tapers down to a fine running butt section that shoots through the guides easily. This allows the line to gain more momentum during a cast, almost as though you were casting a very long, thin sinker. For this reason, it will always give you a longer cast for the same energy. It is excellent for turning over large, wind-resistant flies.

There has been a great deal of improvement in the design of Weight Forward lines in the past five or six years, and there no longer seems any advantage to the Double Taper. The WF profile is becoming the standard, and you might as well begin with it. Your casting will be the better for it.

There are several variations on

the Weight Forward line. The Bass Bug taper carries its weight farther forward, and is designed for casting the larger flies and wind-resistant bass bugs.

The Shooting Taper is a short, 30-foot line tailored for very long distance casting. It is attached to a small diameter monofilament shooting line, and casts farther than any other taper because of reduced resistance through the guides.

Fly lines are also classified according to whether they float or sink.

FLOATING LINES

The floating line is the basic tool of all fly fishing, and is recommended for the beginner. Under the right conditions most game fish (either fresh- or saltwater) will feed near the surface. The floating line is by far the easiest to fish and the most enjoyable to use. Everything is clearly visible to the angler—line, leader, fly, and strike. You can track the line, find the fly at the end of it, and be certain of seeing a strike.

SINKING LINES

Under some circumstances, when the fish are feeding below the surface, you will find it necessary to use sinking lines. An example is when trout are not striking on top, but taking nymphs well under the surface.

Sinking lines come in a range of densities, and are usually classified as Intermediate, Slow Sink, Fast Sink, and Extra-Fast Sink. The choice depends on the water depth at which you want to fish.

Sink rate also depends on current speed and sink time before you start to retrieve. Sink rates are also different in saltwater; the above depths are calculated for freshwater fishing.

THE COMBINATION LINES

As the name implies, the Combination lines are made up partially of a sinking portion (at the front) and a floating portion at the rear. The advantage of the combination line is that it allows you to present your fly at some depth, while still being able to track your line on the surface.

A combination line is also easier to pick up off the water for a backcast, and is easier to "mend" on the surface. (Mending is changing the position of the surface line during a float—the main way of reducing drag on the fly to create a natural appearing drift. See Chapter Six.)

As with full-sinking lines, combination lines come in various lengths, or sinking portions. Your selection depends on depth and type of water to be fished.

The maximum sink rate is achieved only in slack water, or when

Line Type	Depth
Intermediate	In or just below surface film
Slow Sink	Surface film to 5' depth
Fast Sink	Surface film to 15'
Extra-Fast Sink	Surface film to 20'

the line is moving at the same speed as the current. Once you begin to retrieve, the line begins to plane upward.

Seasoned anglers usually carry a

Line Weight	Leader Size	Fly Size
3–5	4X–7X	12–28
6–7	0X–5X	8–22
8–9	2X or larger	4–3/0
10–15	0X or larger	up to 4/0

SINKING LINE

Line Type	Sinking Length
Wet Tip, Fast Sink	10'
Wet Tip, Extra-Fast Sink	20'
Wet Belly, Extra-Fast Sink	30'
Wet Head, Extra-Fast Sink	40'

variety of fly lines to adapt to any condition. However, the beginner should not be intimidated by the great variety available. Details presented here are for your general information and future reference.

SELECTING A FLY LINE

A fly line should be selected on the basis of the type of fishing to be done, the sizes and types of fly to be used, and the rod.

A simple rule: *The lighter the line, the more delicate the presentation. The heavier the line, the easier to cast large flies.*

3–5 weight lines give a light presentation for small flies and spooky trout.

6–7 weight lines are ideally suited for larger, more wind-resistant trout flies under windy conditions. The choice for the angler who fishes primarily with streamers and larger nymphs, and for the bass fisherman who wants more delicacy than power. This weight line will take bass flies size 1 and smaller.

8–9 weight lines are used primarily by trout, salmon, and bass fishermen casting large, wind-resistant flies and bass bugs. Also suitable for lighter saltwater fly fishing.

10–15 weight lines. For those casting very large flies. The choice for saltwater fishing where very long casts are necessary.

FLY LEADER

The purpose of leader is to provide a nearly invisible connection between the fly and the end of the line.

That sounds simple enough. And some fishermen give no more thought to the selection of a leader than that. But in fly fishing, the leader is critically important, perhaps the most important component of the whole "power train" from your hand to the fly, (and, we must hope, the fish.)

As with line, level leader is available, and inexpensive. But also like the level line, it does not perform as well as the tapered variety. There is no use in putting together a finely tuned kit of rod, line, and fly, only to waste it all within 10 feet of the fish.

Tapered leader is the only thing to use. A. J. McClane, when he was fishing editor at *Field and Stream* wrote that, in his opinion, poorly designed leader accounted for 50 percent of the fish that weren't caught.

Think of that for a moment. There is certainly no other part of the fisherman's kit that might account for a 50 percent increase in fish caught!

It is well worth devoting a little extra time to understanding the dynamics of the leader, because it will probably make more difference in your fishing success than any other single factor.

The modern tapered leader is almost like the fly rod itself in construction. It has a butt, a tapered midsection, and a tip portion called the tippet. It can be purchased either as a one-piece length, or with the different sections knotted together. For the sake of simplicity, you will probably want to begin with the unknotted type. Knotted leader has some advantages when you are fine-tuning, but only a fisherman with extensive experience is able to take advantage of them.

This tapered shape performs the same task as does the rod: it delivers the energy of the cast smoothly and controllably. In addition, since it is the part of your line closest to the fish, it has to meet those requirements of near-invisibility as well.

But there is a certain contradiction between what is necessary for the fish, and what is desirable for the fisherman. What makes the best cast is a fairly heavy leader; what makes the best camouflage is the lightest leader possible.

The leader, because of its lightness, plays no significant role in propelling the cast. Indeed, it is some handicap, because it adds drag to the unrolling line.

In order to deliver the fly delicately to the surface, the leader must unroll from the end of the line perfectly straight. An old trick for ensuring that the leader will be straight is to use a 2-inch square of rubber from an inner tube. The leader is drawn through the rubber to stretch it and

---

ANGLER'S HINT

A small piece of rubber inner tube makes an excellent leader straightener.

LEADER SAVVY

Remember that your leader is what comes closest to the fish. Because of that, it is a critical factor in successful fishing, perhaps even more in fly casting than in other forms. Give particular attention to weight and length, and be sure it is not knotted or kinked.

Tippet Size	Pound Test
0X	9.0
1X	7.2
2X	6.3
3X	5.2
4X	4.3
5X	3.3
6X	2.1
7X	1.2

An old trick for insuring that the leader will be straight is to use a 2-inch square of rubber from an inner tube. The leader is drawn through the rubber to stretch it and straighten out any tendency to coil or kink.

Matching leader to fly size is important. The common rule of four can come in handy here.

THE RULE OF FOUR

The hook size divided by four will give you the leader size.
Examples: A size 16 fly divided by four equals a 4X tippet. A size 12 fly would call for a 3X tippet.

straighten out any tendency to coil or kink.

Remember Izaak Walton's friend, Charles Cotton? His two-horsehair tippet would have been about the equivalent of a modern 3X.

Even heavier tippets are available for saltwater fishing. These are classified by pound test, and are available in 6, 10, 12, and 15 pound breaking strength.

Leaders should be coordinated with the type of fly being used, clarity of water, and selectivity of the fish.

Standard commercial leaders today come in lengths of 7½, 9, and 12 feet. The size you want will eventually depend on the fish you are after, and the conditions of your fishing grounds. However, the 9-foot leader is the best general choice.

While the numbers game can get pretty intricate, you will find simple logic will serve you well. Generally speaking, you will want to use a light tippet for small dry flies and nymphs, to allow freedom of movement. Stiffer tippets are recommended for large dries, streamers, and bass bugs.

Part of the behavior of the leader depends on your own style of casting. After you have learned basic casting, the way you deliver energy to the rod will become pretty consistent. At that time, you may want to experiment with designing a leader taper that exactly corresponds to your own style.

As a rough guide to leader design, the following proportions are useful: Butt (approximately two-thirds the diameter of the line point) 60 percent of leader length; Taper 20 percent; and Tippet 20 percent.

While general guidelines are useful, it takes a good deal of trial and error to find the leaders that suit you best. Once you find the right combination for different circumstances, try to maintain consistency whenever you buy leaders. It will pay off handsomely in the end.

BASIC KNOTS

The lore of fisherman's knots is extensive, and can sometimes be confusing. The use of synthetic materials for all lines and leaders changed the craft of knotting dramatically.

Any knot reduces the breaking strength of the line (some by as much as 90 percent). A well-made knot should not only make the necessary connection, but should not reduce breaking strength more than about 20 percent. The knots listed here all meet that criterion.

There are five basic knots that should see you through 99 percent of your needs. These are all relatively easy to tie.

It's a good idea to practice them first with a much heavier material, a stout cord or clothesline. The material is not only easier to handle but will let you see the relationships more clearly than working with the tiny monofilament.

Blood Knot. Used for connecting two lines of fairly similar diameter, as in making tapered leaders or tying new tippet lengths to the leader. You will use this often, as every time you change flies you will lose some of your tippet.

1. Wrap one strand around the other at least four times, then double the end back through the fork between lines.
2. Make the same number of turns with the second strand (in the opposite direction). Then double the second strand back through the opening in the middle of the knot, in the opposite direction from the first strand.
3. Hold the two ends so they don't slip (teeth or fingers). To tighten, slowly

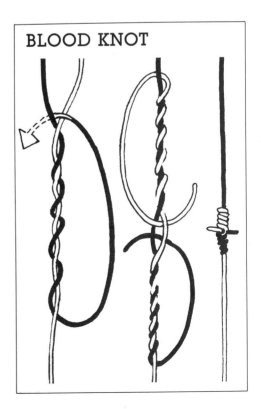

BLOOD KNOT

draw the standing parts in opposite directions. When knot is tight, clip ends.

Perfection End Loop. Used for forming a loop in the end of line or leader.
1. Make one turn around line and hold crossing point between thumb and forefinger.
2. Make a second turn, bringing running end between the two loops formed by the turns.
3. Bring lower loop up *through* upper loop, catching running end between them.
4. To tighten, pull upward on original lower loop, causing original upper loop to tighten around base. Clip.

Improved Clinch Knot. Used to tie flies and bass bugs to leader. A very strong knot.
1. Run the end of the line through the hook eye, and make at least five turns around the standing part.
2. Double back through the opening between the eye and the twists.
3. Pass end through the large loop formed in previous step.
4. To tighten, pull slowly on standing part until knot is snug against hook eye. Clip end.

Surgeon's Knot. Used to connect two lines of very unequal diameter.
1. Place lines parallel with ends pointing in opposite directions.
2. Using the two strands as a single line, make a simple overhand knot, pulling both strands all the way through the loop.
3. Make another overhand knot the same way.
4. To tighten, hold both strands on

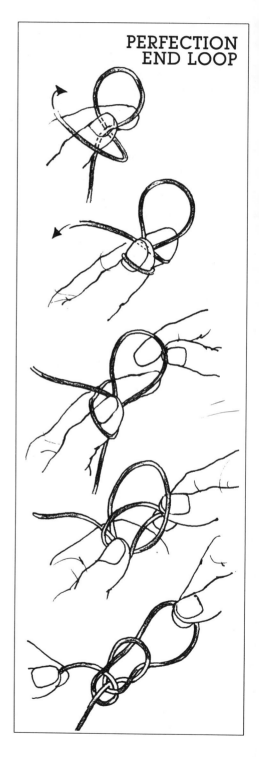

PERFECTION END LOOP

IMPROVED CINCH KNOT

SURGEON'S KNOT

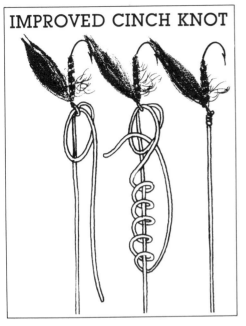

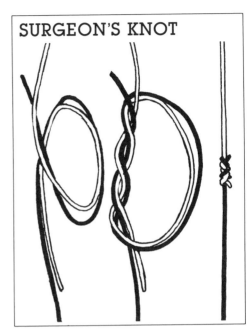

NAIL KNOT

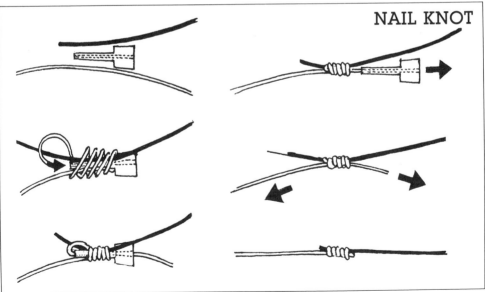

each side of knot, and pull slowly. Clip ends.

Nail Knot. Used for joining butt of leader to end of line, and line to backing. This is a smooth knot that will run easily through the guides. This knot is easiest to tie if you use an inflating needle with the tip cut off, rather than a regular nail.

1. Lay line and leader, pointing in opposite directions, along the inflating needle.
2. Wrap leader back around itself, the fly line, and inflating needle five or six times.
3. Pass running end of leader back *through* the needle tube.
4. Pull both ends of leader to tighten, then remove tube, and complete tightening.
5. Pull on both line and leader to test. Clip ends.

These five basic knots take care of the most general knot requirements. There are other knots that are useful in special circumstances, as well as some variations on the basic repertoire. These are illustrated separately, for your future reference.

For now, if you master the basic five, you will have what you need.

The Duncan Loop. Gives good action because the fly is on a loop and can move independently of the leader. It cinches down to the hook eye as a fish strikes. When fish is released, open the loop a bit for resumption of fishing.

1. Put leader through eye as illustrated.

DUNCAN LOOP UNI-KNOT

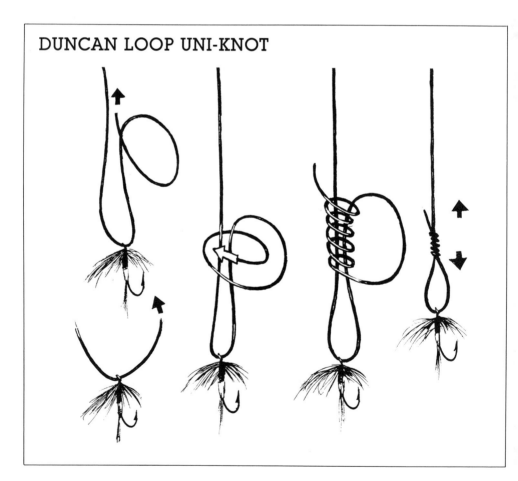

2. Pull through about 8 inches of leader and form a loop as shown.
3. Hold loop and leader in left hand, wrap end of line over the leader.
4. Pass through the loop six times.
5. With end of leader in right hand and fly in left hand, pull with left hand to tighten loop and pull with right hand to snug knot. With left hand thumb and forefinger, slide knot toward fly for desired loop size. Clip.

CHAPTER 4

CLOTHING AND ACCESSORIES

The clothing of the fly fisherman is somewhat specialized, when compared with outdoor wear for camping, hunting, or hiking. The angler is a creature partly of the land and partly of the water, and this ambiguity imposes a special set of demands.

Over the years both the design and materials of fly fishing garb have undergone a steady evolution. The major changes, of course, have occurred with the introduction of new synthetic fabrics.

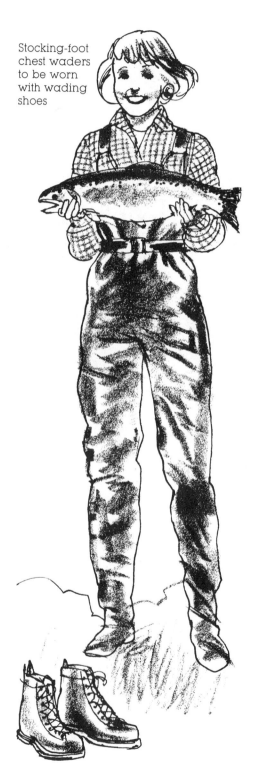

Stocking-foot chest waders to be worn with wading shoes

There is an amusing irony in the fact that there is no sport that brings you closer to nature, and there is no sport that has gotten more benefit from synthetic, high-tech materials.

WADERS

While much good fishing is possible from the bank of a stream, or from boats, you will extend your possibilities greatly with a pair of waders. Waders increase your range so dramatically that they could almost be considered a form of transportation, rather than clothing.

While hip boots have some application in small streams, particularly on the Eastern Seaboard, there is not much question that your first purchase should be chest waders. The same logic that gets you into waders in the first place would indicate that your scope will be vastly extended with chest waders.

Today, the typical wader is made of a high-count nylon taffeta with either urethane or butyl rubber coatings inside. Recent years have also seen the introduction of neoprene waders, with material similar to underwater diving gear, which have proven very successful in cold waters.

There are basically two types of chest waders available on the current

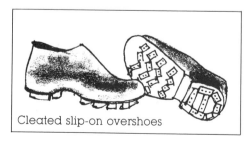

Cleated slip-on overshoes

market. (1) Boot-foot waders, in which the wading shoe is an integral part of the wader, and (2) stocking-foot waders, which require a separate wading shoe.

Your choice will depend on what kind of fishing you do (and how you get there.) If you want to go lightweight—for example, backpacking into high mountain streams or lakes— you will probably want stocking-foot waders.

In the past few years a new breed of "flyweight" waders has appeared, so light they can be balled up and put in a pocket of your fishing vest.

The main disadvantage here is that you trade one kind of convenience for another. Stocking-foot waders require that you first put on the wader, then stockings over that, and finally a wading shoe. You are more subject to loose gravel creeping into your shoes, and the shoe stays wet after you take it off.

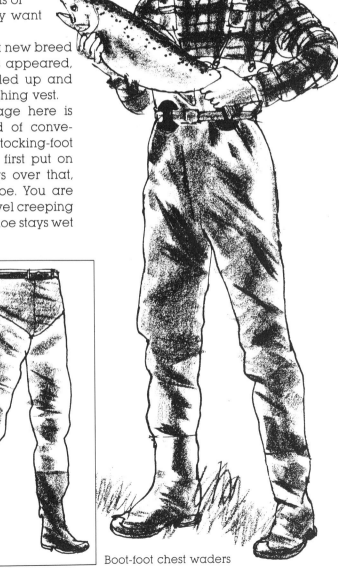

Hip boots

Boot-foot chest waders

Boot-foot waders are more bulky to begin with, but you can just slip them on and off. Because the boot is an integral part of the wader itself, gravel is not a problem.

The sole of the wading shoe, whether attached or separate, is of critical importance. The two basic kinds of sole are cleated and felt (and they are sometimes combined).

Wading cleats are either molded of hard rubber, like a hiking shoe, or aluminum studs. They may either be a part of the wader itself, or come in the form of a rubber slipper that fits over the bottom of your shoe.

In the smooth-bed limestone streams of the Southeast, a cleated shoe is excellent. However, for free-stone streambeds like those of the Pacific Northwest and New England, a felt sole without cleats is preferable.

The moss and algae growth in rocky streambeds can be as slippery as any black ice, and the angler can quickly find himself sitting down when he thought he was standing up. The felt sole gives very much better traction in those circumstances.

The felt sole should probably be considered the standard for most parts of the country, unless you find that the majority of anglers in your area use cleats.

OUTFITTING TIPS

Waders need care! Dry them slowly, not too near a source of heat. Stuffing with newspapers is a good way to absorb inside moisture. Always hang upside down from the boot. How long they last will depend on how you care for them.

Of the many dozens of fishing vest patterns, you will certainly be able to find one that suits you. It all depends on how well a particular vest suits *your* sense of order. The maximum number of pockets doesn't necessarily mean the greatest convenience.

If the majority of your fishing is wading, a short jacket will suit you best in the long run, as the skirts will not trail in the water. If most of your fishing is from the bank or a boat, the long parka offers better protection around the hips.

A comfortable, protective hat can add more to your comfort than any other accessory. It is a necessity in *any* kind of weather. Be sure it is absolutely comfortable as you'll be wearing it hour after hour. A lining that is too tight or stiff can drive you crazy by the end of the day.

Polarized sunglasses give you a window into the world below the surface. Even if you do not wear sun glasses normally, *wear these*. It is not a matter of protecting your eyes from glare (though they also do that), as much as it is extending your vision. Polarized glasses are a fly fishing *tool*, as much as your hook.

WADERS NEED CARE!

Their lifespan will depend on how you use them (or abuse them). None of them, sad to say, will last forever. One fisherman may get five seasons out of a pair of waders, while another will have them torn to pieces in a few weeks.

Waders are impervious to water. They are definitely not impervious to blackberries, brush, or barbed wire. A patching kit is a necessity, but your only real insurance is the care you give them. These three simple rules will help you extend the life of your waders.

1. Watch where you walk.
2. Dry waders immediately after use.
3. Hang them up by the boot.

Wear long underwear under your waders

UNDERWEAR

Heat loss is a significant problem when standing in a cold stream perhaps for hours at a time. Full-length underwear beneath your waders is a necessity.

Here is one area in which natural fibers still have an edge. While some synthetics such as polypropylene have excellent insulating properties, there are none that have the "wicking" property of natural wool. Wool actually draws moisture into itself, keeping adjacent surfaces dry. Natural wool can absorb 90 percent of its own weight in water before it loses any of its insulating properties.

There are three materials to choose from in picking underwear.

1. All wool. Ultimately, this is probably the best *if* you can wear it comfortably. Some people can tolerate it, some can't. It is also somewhat more expensive than either blends or synthetics.
2. The Duofold type, consisting of a cotton inner layer for the sake of comfort, and a wool outer layer for insulation and wicking.
3. Polypropylene. This is an excellent synthetic. It maintains its insulating loft when wet, as does wool, but lacks the property of absorbing moisture to the same degree. It is now considerably less expensive than wool.

The same considerations apply to choosing socks. All-wool with a cotton inner sock will be most effective in keeping your feet both dry and warm. The wool will wick the moisture out of the cotton sock, keeping it, and your feet, dry.

FISHING VEST

The vest is really the key to fly fishing accessories, and it is one of the most personal items in any fisherman's kit. If you ask ten equally expert fly fishermen to design a fishing vest, you will end up with ten totally different vests.

The basic requirement, however, is relatively simple. It has to carry everything you need. The ideal fly fishing vest has been described as an infinity of pockets held together with a couple of seams. Regardless of the merits of any specific design, that is approximately what they all are.

Any vest will have from 6 to 25 pockets, variously arranged. The major difference is between the full vest, and the shorty, wading vest.

The shorty vest is the best first choice. It is more than discouraging to look down and find that all the lower pockets of your vest are underwater. The shorty vest makes it possible to wade to the full depth your waders allow, without worrying.

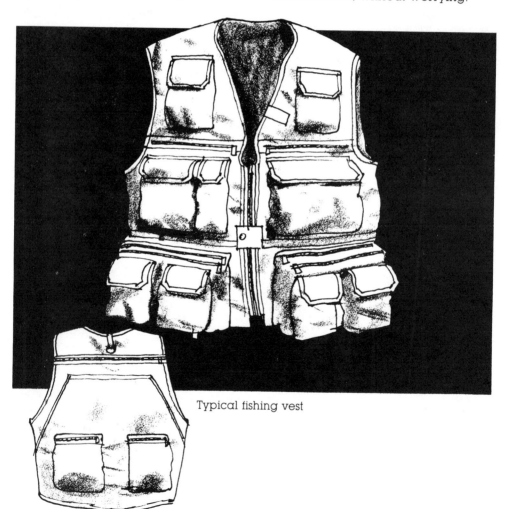

Typical fishing vest

Short wading jacket

RAIN JACKETS

New synthetic materials like Gore-Tex have made a change here. Your choice will be between a conventional nylon jacket with a waterproof rubber coating, and one of the new materials.

As with your fishing vest, length is a consideration here, and for the same reasons. A short jacket will probably serve you better in wading circumstances than a full-length parka.

The nylon jacket is equally waterproof, and has the advantage that it can be stuffed in the cargo pocket of your vest when you are not using it. However, it suffers from the problem of condensation, and particularly when it is worn over a pair of waders. It is possible to get as wet from your own condensed perspiration as from the rain.

Gore-Tex, on the other hand, deals very well with condensation. The pores of the fabric are far too small to allow liquid water to pass through, but large enough that water vapor readily escapes to the outside without condensing.

The earliest versions of Gore-Tex were rather stiff and "crinkly," but this has improved a good deal. We are now in about the third generation of Gore-Tex-like materials, and if you haven't looked at them lately, it will be worth your while. They are still slightly heavier and stiffer than the

Down vest under
chest waders

nylon, but on the whole this is out-weighed by their better performance.

First choice in a rain jacket would be a shorty jacket of a Gore-Tex-like material, of which there are several on the market under different brand names.

DOWN VEST

In cold weather, nothing is better for extra insulation than a light down vest worn under your waders. A vest is preferable to a full-sleeved jacket, in that it leaves your arms completely free. In combination with a shorty rain jacket, you're prepared for almost any weather.

GLOVES

Designing gloves for the angler presents a number of special problems because the requirements are contradictory.

In addition to keeping his hands and fingers warm, the fly fisherman needs to have full, or nearly full, sensitivity in his fingers. Trying to knot tip-pet, or tie a new fly to your line, is about as clumsy with heavy gloves as with cold fingers. The result is that the normal angler's gloves come off rather frequently.

There have been several interesting approaches to the problem. Some outfitters supply a finger-free glove.

This type of glove leaves the last joint of the finger free. Sometimes all the fingers, sometimes only the thumb and forefinger.

The warmest are made of neoprene, and fit very snugly around the fingers, preventing water from dripping back down inside.

Interestingly, the fingertips remain much warmer if the wrists are kept warm. The blood supplying the fingers passes through the wrist fairly close to the surface, and if that area is kept warm, the fingers can tolerate much more cold. If you opt for a finger-free glove, be sure that is reaches well up on the wrist.

Steelheaders on the Pacific Coast have a homemade solution. They wear a pair of light wool glove liners for warmth, and over the top pull a lightweight surgical glove. The surgical glove both waterproofs the whole thing, and provides a sensitive touch.

THE HAT

There is a lot of humor based on the fisherman's devotion to his favorite hat. But make no mistake, your hat is one of the most essential pieces of equipment you have.

In these days when the average urban male only walks from his house to the car and from the car to his office, hats are no longer as universally used as they once were. But the simple hat is probably the most effective climate-modifying device ever invented by man. The bare head is extremely sensitive to heat, cold, and wet, and it is folly to go fishing without a hat that both fits well and serves its purpose.

For summer fishing, the "Florida fishing hat" serves well. It has a generous visor in front as a sunshield and a flap in back that protects the back of the neck and ears.

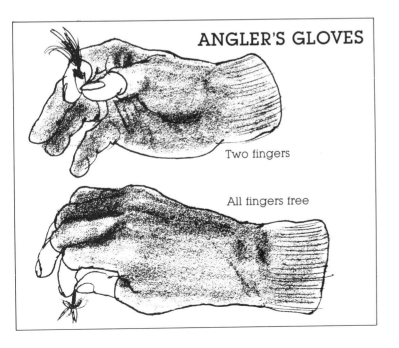

ANGLER'S GLOVES

Two fingers

All fingers free

But undoubtedly the favorite, and most practical, headgear is a wide-brimmed felt hat. On Western streams, some variety of cowboy hat is most often seen.

Any wide-brimmed hat will do, as long as it protects both your face and the back of your neck. And protection is needed from more than the weather: There are days in every angler's life when that needle-sharp hook has an irresistible attraction to the back of your neck. Flies have also been known to mistake a naked ear for a trout, and give it a little nip. The result is very painful, and only too humorous to your fellow anglers. Better is should happen to your hat.

Many fly fishermen use a hatband of lamb's wool, which provides a convenient place to hook flies if you don't want to be going in and out of your fly boxes all the time.

ACCESSORIES

POLARIZED SUNGLASSES
The number-one necessary accessory is a good pair of polarized sunglasses. Nothing will make more difference in reading water. They are one of the most important tools the fisherman can have, and should be the first thing you pick up and hang around your neck.

ANGLER'S HINT

A sheepskin hat band is a handy place to secure flies. It is also convenient when you want to carry only a few flies and not the whole arsenal associated with a vest.

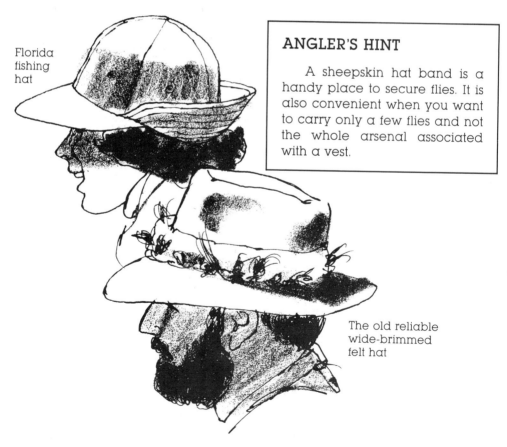

Florida fishing hat

The old reliable wide-brimmed felt hat

Polarized sunglasses are an underwater window

The ability to see beneath the surface of the water will be a help to you a thousand times a day. For example, if the fish are nymphing, taking the insect just as it emerges from the nymph stage, you will have no way of knowing why they are not striking your dry fly. The polarized glasses will let you see the flash of a turning belly, and clue you to what is happening.

SURGICAL FORCEPS

An all-round indispensable tool for the fly fisherman. On a well-hooked fish you can sometimes have a great deal of difficulty getting the hook free without injuring the fish. With forceps, you simply clamp the fly, and the fish can be shaken loose comparatively easily. They also serve the same purpose in pulling flies out of your clothing (and yourself).

ANGLER'S HINT

In discolored water, after a rain or high water, streamers are an excellent choice.

KNOT TYERS

Several small tools are available on the market to help in the fussy job of tying knots. Tying knots in the field can be quite a different experience from practicing in your living room, and a frustrating one.

For tying the often-used nail knot, a handy improvised tool is an inflating needle of the kind used for volleyballs or basketballs.

Even if you have perfect vision, it is a great help to have some kind of needle-threading device for thread-

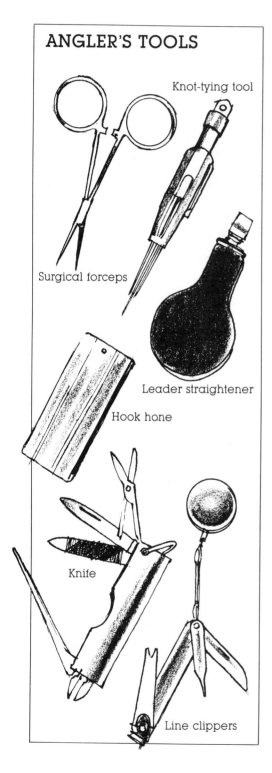

ANGLER'S TOOLS

Knot-tying tool

Surgical forceps

Leader straightener

Hook hone

Knife

Line clippers

ing the tippet to the fly. Several of the knot-tying tools incorporate a threader of some kind.

Don't worry that using a "gadget" for tying knots will brand you a hopeless newcomer. Long-experienced fishermen use them, and even if they didn't, you should. A great deal depends on a properly tied knot.

Every knot diminishes the strength of the line to some degree, ranging from about 20 percent to as much as 90 percent. A badly tied knot is a big disadvantage, and it can be immensely frustrating to have trout rising to a hatch before your eyes while you are fumbling with a pesky knot.

HOOK HONE

Few fishermen believe that any hook comes from the factory sharp enough, and a hook sharpener is another essential. Again, several brands of commercial hook sharpeners are available, but you will find you can do as good a job with an automotive file used for dressing points.

ANGLER'S HINT

All hooks should be sharpened before fishing.

LEADER STRAIGHTENER

These are small, gum rubber pads used for straightening the kinks and coils out of leader. The commercial varieties may cost $7 or $8, and a 2-inch square of inner-tube rubber will do as well.

You will also need a small, *sharp* knife, and a pair of clippers or small scissors.

These gadgets can be a nuisance to find by rummaging through the pockets of your vest. The easy way to carry them is on the kind of small key-keeper with a retractable chain. Your outfitter has many of these tools available mounted on a tiny "retrieve-it" reel. You simply pin the reel to your vest, which keeps the tool both easily available and out of the way.

FLOATANTS AND MUD

These substances perform opposite functions. The purpose of the floatant material is to waterproof your fly, keeping it on the surface when dry-fly fishing. Mud lets it sink, for wet-fly or nymphing. Both can be found with automatic "retrieve-its" of the key-keeper type.

This is a somewhat abbreviated list of all the various accessories available, but covers the essentials. They all have the same purpose, to make your fishing more pleasurable and effective.

FLY TYING EQUIPMENT

There are few top-flight fishermen who do not tie their own flies, at least from time to time. In addition to being useful in the sport, fly tying is an enjoyable and rewarding hobby in its own right. On winter days with the snow piled up outside, nothing brings to mind the delights of fishing your favorite stream like tying the flies to do it with.

The literature and lore of fly tying is as vast as that of the fishing itself, and you can carry it to any degree of sophistication and knowledge. One

standard reference lists 5,400 different ties, so the resource is nearly limitless.

It is true that a fly that might cost $1.50 commercially can be made for about a dime, which rates your personal time as zero. It is also true that you can tie that extra-special design of your own that will undoubtedly catch fish when nothing else does.

But neither the economics nor the efficiency is the real reason behind the growing numbers of fly tying hobbyists. The real reason is—it's an awful lot of fun.

The basic tools of fly tying are simple and quite inexpensive. Several suppliers provide a basic set of tools for under $40.

The principal materials are feathers, fur, fabric, tinsel, and hooks—all in a bewildering profusion. To begin with, you should purchase a selection of materials put together as a beginner's kit. As you develop your skills, you can add specialized materials when you see you need them. A kit, available either by mail or from your local tackle shop, will get you started.

ANGLER'S HINT

Fingernail clippers can be used to pinch down barbs on small fly hooks.

You can save an enormous amount of time and wasted effort by taking a class in fly tying. Such classes are given by many tackle shops, sportsmen's clubs, YMCA's, and professional fly tyers. You should have no difficulty locating one in your area.

These are the basic tools you will need.

FLY TYING MATERIALS

VISE

The fly tying vise is a lever-and-cam device used to hold the hook securely while you work on the fly. A single

movement of the lever will grasp or release the hook, making it very easy to deal with. The vise tip will generally swivel and point in any direction for ease of use (as well as allowing you to see your work from all angles). The vise conveniently clamps to the edge of your work table, and can easily be brought out for an evening's work.

While it is much easier to work with a fly tying vise, it is worth noting that many a good fly has been tied with no more than a C-clamp to hold the hook, and another to clamp the clamp to your table.

HACKLE PLIERS

Hackle pliers can be purchased either with rubber jaws, or "English" style, with plain metal jaws. When the plier is squeezed, the jaws are opened. They are used to hold the hackle securely as it is wound around the shank of the hook.

The only reasonable substitute for hackle pliers is the surgeon's forceps, which are already a part of your field kit. They do a good job, but, again, are not as convenient to use. Since the commercial hackle pliers cost very little, it makes sense to have them.

SCISSORS

The main auxiliary tool is a good pair of small scissors, with either straight or curved blades. They are used for cutting thread and other dressing materials. Occasionally a larger pair will be useful in making hair bugs.

DUBBING NEEDLE

The dubbing needle is a rather heavy, very sharp steel needle set in a wood or plastic handle. It has a

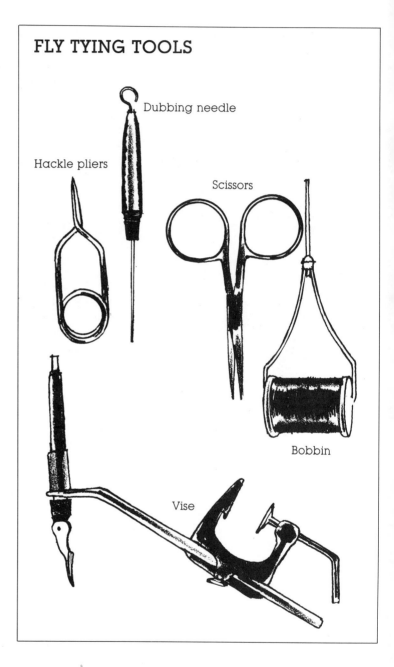

FLY TYING TOOLS

Dubbing needle

Hackle pliers

Scissors

Bobbin

Vise

myriad uses, including separating strands of floss, picking out hair bodies to make them fuzzier, dividing wings, and the like. You will find it in your hand as often as any other tool.

BOBBIN
The bobbin is not only a device for holding the spool of tying thread, but provides a necessary tension as it hangs down from the hook while you

are working. Tying thread is very fine, and easily abraded by rough fingertips, leading to a weaker tie. Using a bobbin prevents this, as well as saving thread.

Though there are many other useful tools available (everything from hackle guards to a magnifying glass) the tools presented here are the basics. Mastery of these tools will make your fly tying more efficient and certainly more pleasurable.

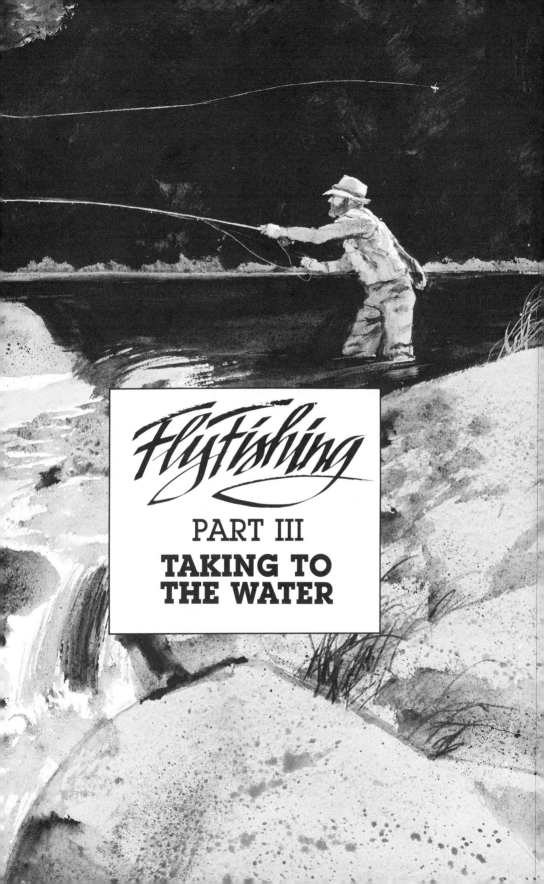

Flyfishing

PART III

TAKING TO THE WATER

CHAPTER 5

FLIES AND FLY TYING

There is a simple rule of thumb that might have saved tens of thousands of words of disputation about artificial flies: It doesn't matter in the least what a fly looks like to you, the fisherman. It matters what it looks like to the fish.

That is not always easy to determine, of course. The world of the fish is very different from yours, and the same logic does not apply. It is safe to say that not one out of ten thousand fishermen ever tries to look at the world from the perspective of the fish. Yet that reversed perspective is the most powerful tool for catching fish ever devised.

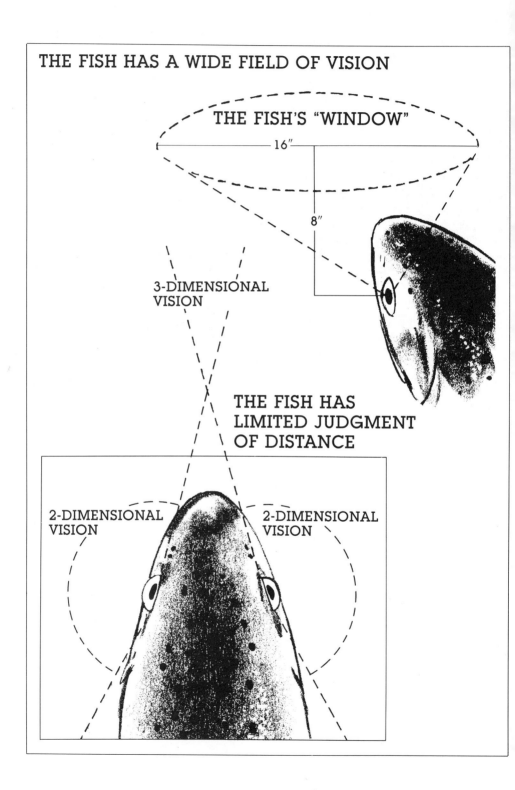

THE FISH HAS A WIDE FIELD OF VISION

THE FISH'S "WINDOW"

16"

8"

3-DIMENSIONAL
VISION

THE FISH HAS
LIMITED JUDGMENT
OF DISTANCE

2-DIMENSIONAL
VISION

2-DIMENSIONAL
VISION

The fish's field of vision is very wide. Because of the side placement of the eyes, a fish can see in virtually every direction except straight down and straight back. However, he can judge distance only in the narrow triangle where the field of both eyes overlaps. (See illustration.)

When looking upward toward the surface of his world, the fish sees through a rather narrow circular "window" in a mirrored ceiling. This window to the air world is only about twice the diameter of his depth. That is, if the fish is lying at an 8-inch depth, the window through which he sees is only 16 inches across. The rest of the ceiling is reflecting his underwater world.

A fly that floats across this window

ANGLER'S HINT

In bright sunlight, fish shaded areas.

---

will appear as a series of bright dimples in the surface, with a more or less distorted silhouette of the fly's body, seen against the bright sky. The degree of distortion depends on how smooth the water surface is.

It is not a lot to go on, if that is how you make your living. So the fish also uses color and movement as clues to tell him whether this is in fact a meal, or merely stream flotsam.

The fish shares his world with a wide variety of other aquatic creatures, of which the most important from the fisherman's point of view are the aquatic insects that provide the bulk of most fishes' food.

These insects, in their various stages of life, are more familiar to the fish than your next door neighbors are to you. They are intimately known to him, as part and parcel of the cycle of stream life. The surprise is not that so many fish are *not* caught but that any are caught by such deception.

If you give a little thought to understanding the cycle of an aquatic insect's life, your understanding of the various kinds of artificial flies will fall into place automatically.

The vast majority of the insect's life is spent underwater. The female deposits her fertilized eggs, usually from the air. They sink to the bottom of the stream, adhering to rocks, twigs, grasses, logs, almost anything.

The eggs hatch out into small nymphs, which immediately form hard nymphal cases in which they can grow. As they develop, they trade one case for another, and from the point of view of the insect, this is the main portion of their lives, lasting sometimes for several years, hidden beneath the surface, invisible to us.

But then, finally, there is a change. A sudden change, a picking up of the pace of life. The nymph begins to swim about, finally swimming up to the surface, where the last nymphal case splits, and the miraculously transformed creature emerges as a winged insect. This is called the "dun" stage. It is what the fisherman sees when a "hatch" is on.

This weak, partly formed dun flutters on the surface, makes short flights toward shore, falls back, flies again. Those who eventually make it to dry land, develop quickly into mature flies, and this is called the "spinner" stage.

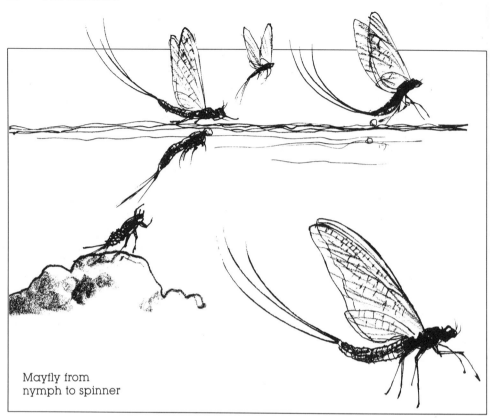

Mayfly from
nymph to spinner

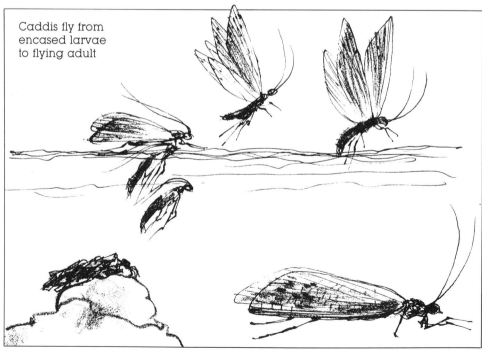

Caddis fly from
encased larvae
to flying adult

Not all flies go through these stages in the same way. The stonefly nymph, for example, crawls out on the land before beginning to shuck the nymphal case, and its dun phase occurs on land.

Compared to the slow years beneath the water, its airborne life is pitifully short. It has come into this strange world for one purpose only, to breed. It is all over in a flash of time, and the adult insect may live only twenty-four hours, or at most a few days.

The fertilized female returns to the water to deposit her eggs. Then she dies, wings flat, in the "spent-wing" stage, and the cycle begins again.

What we see from shore is only a flashing glimpse of the most ephemeral portion of the fly's life. And, in fact, the genus of the mayfly is *Ephemeroptera*, the "short-lived fly."

With this life cycle in mind, it is easy to see what is represented—to the fish—by the fly you cast.

The nymph is represented by the artificial nymph, the struggling dun that has drowned is the wet fly, the surviving dun or spinner is represented by the dry fly.

In the field of direct imitation, what remains is to match your deception with the actual insect in size, color, movement, and so forth.

While every stream or lake naturally has a unique population of aquatic insects, the three that concern the fly fisherman most are the mayfly, the stonefly, and the caddis fly. Most of the traditional artificial flies are imitations of one of those three in one of its stages.

This all makes a good deal of sense, even has a reasonably scien-

Stonefly Dun
emerges on land

tific, rational ring to it. But fishing, fortunately or unfortunately, is not entirely a rational matter.

This scenario, for example, does not explain why some of the best fishing flies in the world bear no close resemblance to *any* known insect. The Royal Coachman, with its scarlet midbody and green and blue peacock iridescence, doesn't look like any known insect, and yet is one of the most successful patterns ever tied. It was first tied (literally) by the Royal Coachman of England, and the colors are the traditional Coachman's colors! We must assume the trout knows nothing of all this.

This variety of fly, resembling no particular insect—or perhaps resembling them all at the same time—is classified as an "Attractor," as opposed to an "Imitator." The theory goes that the fish is attracted by a specific flash of color, a dash of ex-

citement in an otherwise dull day on the eating job.

This may be true. Like many theories, particularly about fly fishing, it is designed to cover the fact that our first theory doesn't always work.

This example is given to clarify another rule of thumb you will dis-

---

ANGLER'S HINT

The most inexpensive way to experiment with fly tying is to buy the tools in kit form. Some dealers provide an excellent assortment of materials in their kits, as well. The specialized tools are the vise and bobbin—you can usually improvise the others from materials around the house.

TACKLE TIPS

The fisherman's secret weapon is the ability to think like the fish. If you do not have some understanding of the life cycle of the fish (and his food), you handicap yourself severely. A little time spent in learning about the world from the perspective of the fish will make more difference in your success than any amount of equipment.

The Art of Imitation. Imitator flies represent specific phases in the life cycle of the insect:

1. The dry fly = the mature insect, the "spinner."

2. The wet fly = a drowned fly, or one not yet flown.
3. The nymph = the larval stage, before emergence.
4. Streamers = small baitfish.
5. Terrestrials = land insects blown into water.

Attractors. This kind of fly does not mimic any specific insect. Often brightly colored, it is thought they attract the attention of the fish through brightness and movement. Some attractors (such as the Royal Coachman) are among the best fish-getters of all.

cover almost immediately as you enter the sport: *Nobody's theory works all the time.*

The fish is the only real authority. If you get the word from a fish, take it. If you get the word from a fisherman, take it with a grain of salt.

With that disclaimer, let's look at the flies you will be using.

DRY FLIES—THE BASIC SET

The dry fly imitates a natural insect *floating* on the surface.

This is emphasized because remembering it may be more important to catching fish than the fly pattern you choose.

A fish is exquisitely sensitive to every motion of the water. He "works" his water every second of his life. The current brings him food, provides him with a place to rest, determines where he will be at any given moment. It is the most important single element in his life, and he makes no mistakes about it.

If your fly is moving even fractionally differently from the prevailing current at that point, the fish will have nothing to do with it. It is obviously something foreign, no matter how much it may physically *look* like something he knows. We will deal more fully with this in Chapter Six. For now, bear in mind that the presentation of the fly is at least as important as the pattern.

The contents of your dry-fly box depend on what you are fishing for, where you are fishing, and the size of your bank account. With thousands of patterns to choose from, the bank ac-

count can be a pretty significant factor, even at $1.50 apiece.

Most top-flight fishermen will admit you can do pretty well with a selection of only four or five basic patterns. A. J. McClane, in his excellent book *The Practical Fly Fisherman*, lists these as enough to begin with!

A. J. McClane's List
1. A bivisible
2. A spider
3. A bunched wing pattern
4. A fly with white wings, visible at dusk

Dan Bailey's eminent tackle shop in Livingston, Montana, puts up a coast-to-coast selection that he estimates is good for trout about 90 percent of the time.

Dan Bailey's List
1. Adams
2. Light Cahill
3. Quill Gordon
4. Hendrickson

The late Joe Brooks listed his ten "consistent fish getters everywhere" as:

Joe Brooks's List
1. Light Cahill
2. Adams
3. Quill Gordon
4. Gray Midge Hackle Fly
5. Black Flying Ant
6. Red Variant
7. Black Gnat
8. Gray Wulff
9. Blue Dun
10. Jassid

Cam Sigler's list of the best half-dozen dry flies for general use is:

Adams

Royal Coachman

Light Cahill

Gray Hackle Peacock

Black Gnat

Ginger Quill

Cam's Half-Dozen

1. Adams
2. Royal Coachman
3. Light Cahill
4. Gray Hackle Peacock
5. Black Gnat
6. Ginger Quill

For the Western angler, the following more specialized assortment may prove useful:

1. Irresistible
2. Rat-faced McDougal
3. Humpy
4. Sofa Pillow
5. Troth Elk-Hair Caddis
6. Royal Wulff

Whatever your selection, you will need at least three of each, which is about the minimum for a day's trip. For trips longer than a single day, you will need proportionately more.

You will eventually want to broaden your selection of patterns, of course. But in the beginning it is probably more important to have a selection of sizes in the basic patterns, rather than adding new patterns.

The most common size is probably a 16, representing a midpoint between the smaller and larger flies.

Sizes 12, 14, and 16 are good general sizes, while an 18 or 20 in the smaller flies is useful. Many novices shy away from the smaller sizes, but they will sometimes produce results where nothing else works. A change of size will catch fish about as often as a change of pattern.

The most useful size ultimately depends on local conditions, and your best bet is advice from your tackle shop and local anglers.

FISHING THE DRY FLY

The standard rule for fishing dry flies

Irresistible

Rat-faced McDougal

Humpy

Sofa Pillow

Troth Elk-Hair Caddis

Royal Wulff

is to fish upstream. Fish face upstream into the current, looking for food to come down to them from above. It is much easier to approach a fish from behind or below without spooking him. Still, use caution and wade softly and quietly with no sharp, fast movements.

When fishing any stream, notice the main runs and spots that are natural drifts for flies riding the surface. Also fish the secondary runs, undercut banks, and the tops and bottoms of pools. Be especially cautious in late evening, for fish move into the shallows to cruise and look for insects.

When you see fish rising, pick the closest one and cast to him. Don't just cast blind into a pool of feeding fish; pick one as your target. Watch the rise of a fish and cast above it. The ring from a rising fish moves downstream, so it can be deceptive. Present the fly above the fish and float it downstream over him.

The best tied flies are ineffective if they do not float freely on the surface and look natural. Therefore, you must reduce line drag as much as possible. It is important to learn the S-cast (see Chapter Six), and how to mend line.

When fishing heavily rippled water, the larger flies can be effective. Fish in fast, rough water are not as selective, and the larger flies are easily seen. If you lose sight of the fly in rough water, follow the line to the end and track the leader in the water to the fly.

Although the upstream rule is a good one, dry flies are also fished downstream. Many times trout will rise below you after you have covered an area. The best approach is to cast above a downstream fish using the S-cast to avoid drag and get the fly out in front of the fly line so it drifts down to the fish without the line spooking him.

Also be aware that when a fish takes your fly downstream, he's facing you. Give him time to take the fly completely, to avoid pulling it out of his mouth.

WET FLIES— THE BASIC SET

The wet fly, imitating a drowned natural, is fished below the surface. How far below? That is the crux of wet-fly fishing, and a question impossible to answer, because it depends entirely on the particular conditions of the stream and how the fish are feeding.

Wet-fly fishing is the oldest form of fly fishing. Our Macedonian angler was using a wet fly, and Dame Juliana Berners' patterns were all wet flies. The dry fly came along only in the middle of the last century.

It is now thought that the wet fly is often mistaken for a nymph, rather than a drowned adult insect. Unless the fish 'fess up, we'll probably never know. Fishermen, at least, seem to think so, as wet flies are sold less and less and nymphs are on the increase. And it is certainly the case that 70 to 80 percent of the fishes' diet consists of insects in the nymph stage. Still, there are times when only the wet fly will produce.

There are a number of popular fly patterns that can be fished either wet or dry, such as the Light Cahill and the Royal Coachman. Usually the difference is only in whether the wings are tied upright to simulate a living fly, or parallel to the body to simulate a drowned one. Hence the duplications in the lists below.

CAM'S HALF-DOZEN WET FLIES

Royal Coachman

Hare's Ear (gold-ribbed)

March Brown

Light Cahill

Blue Dun

Adams (tied wet, wings down)

Joe Brooks's Basic List
1. Gray Hackle, Yellow body
2. Brown Hackle
3. Coachman
4. Royal Coachman
5. Black Gnat
6. Quill Gordon
7. Blue Dun
8. Light Cahill
9. March Brown
10. Ginger Quill

Cam's Half-Dozen
1. Royal Coachman
2. Hare's Ear (gold-ribbed)
3. March Brown
4. Light Cahill
5. Blue Dun
6. Adams (tied wet, wings down)

FISHING THE WET FLY

The most common technique for fishing the wet fly is the cross-stream cast, casting the fly a bit upstream and across, and retrieving in short jerks interspersed with longer strips of the line. Another method is the free float, which is accomplished by casting across stream, then letting the fly float free in the current, occasionally giving a few short attracting jerks.

Whichever method you use, it is important to get the longest possible natural free float. Fish will often follow a wet fly to the end of the swing and hold in behind it. Once the fly has swung in below you, it is a good practice to retrieve with a few short jerks before picking it out of the water. This will often induce a fish hanging behind to hit with a bang.

When fishing the larger pools, start your casts well up in the head of the pool and close in and cover the area completely. Then move downstream and fish the same method.

When fishing a pool, move slowly and deliberately, remembering your quarry is facing upstream.

When fishing the wet fly upstream, use the same method as with the dry fly, picking your spots carefully. Use short casts for better control, and retrieve the fly at the speed of the current so it looks like a natural fly drifting with the current.

One additional basic rule of wet-fly fishing is very important. *Watch the line.* Since you cannot see the fly, it is more difficult to detect a strike, so if the line slows or stops, pay attention! It may be just a rock on the bottom, but it could be that trophy fish you're looking for.

NYMPHS

Nymphs have been steadily growing in popularity over the past few years. In the West there are certainly more nymph patterns sold than traditional wet flies.

Even during spectacular hatches, when the air over a stream seems to be a cloud of dancing mayflies, the fish will sometimes not strike even a perfect dry fly. And yet, you can see them feeding, the water bulging all around you.

That bulge is the clue to what is happening just below the surface. You will remember the fly's life cycle: at the last moment the nymph becomes a free-swimming creature and moves up to the surface to hatch into the dun stage.

When the feeding fish bulges the water without breaking the surface, he is nymphing. Or, strictly speaking, he is taking the "emergers" just as the nymphal shell is discarded.

While there are many details of a fish's feeding that may seem rather obscure to us, there is a certain clear logic that is never violated. Mother nature is magnificently bountiful in her creations, but there is always a certain efficiency of style.

All living creatures, including us, face a trade-off between energy expended and energy taken in. The fish, by his very nature, will be trying to take in as much food as possible with the minimum expenditure of energy.

This principle of efficiency undoubtedly makes the nymph a better bargain. Once a mayfly has reached the dun stage, it can fly and flutter, and it has become something at the very edge of the fishes' world. The nymph is less mobile, has less chance of escape, and is still wholly beneath the water.

The list published by Joe Brooks concentrates on flies tied by Eastern tyers, where nymph fishing has a somewhat longer history than in the West.

Joe Brooks's List
1. Light Stonefly
2. Yellow Mayfly
3. March Brown
4. Tellico
5. Ginger Quill
6. Brown Drake
7. Black and Yellow
8. Orange and Black
9. Black
10. Ed Burke

All of these are tied on sizes 10 to 14. In the West, there are some much larger nymphs, like those of the Western Stonefly, which may be so large they are tied on a size 6 long shank hook.

CAM'S HALF-DOZEN NYMPHS

Stonefly nymph

Hare's-Ear nymph (Caddis)

Gray nymph

Montana nymph

Beaver nymph

Zug Bug

Cam's Half-Dozen
1. Stonefly
2. Hare's-Ear Nymph (caddis)
3. Gray Nymph
4. Montana Nymph
5. Beaver Nymph
6. Zug Bug

FISHING THE NYMPH

When there is no hatch visible and attractor dry flies are not producing fish, they may be feeding on nymphs. Even when there is a visible hatch, telltale rings and ripples indicate fish are feeding under the hatch, but even the best imitation fly cannot produce a strike.

When the fish are bulging, fish upstream with a high floating line, so that the nymph floats just under the surface. Cast above the fish, and free float the nymph just as you would a dry fly. Keep an eye on the line; if it pauses, stops, or moves forward, a fish has picked it up.

On days when dry flies, wet flies, and streamers are all unproductive, yet you can see fish flashing and moving down deep, they are probably nymphing on the bottom. To fish them in this situation, tie on a nymph and cast upstream. Play out line so the nymph will sink deep, let the fly float free, and watch the line carefully for strikes. It is a good idea to cast higher above the fish than usual, in order to give time for the nymph to sink.

It is also productive to fish nymphs using an across-stream cast, letting the nymph float naturally across and down below you. Retrieve a few feet before you pick up the line from the water.

In slow, still water, a jerky retrieve fished across stream can produce well.

Trout feeding
on surface

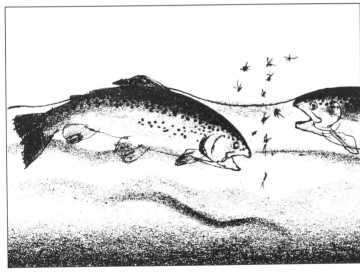

Trout
bulging

STREAMERS AND BUCKTAILS

With streamers and bucktails we enter a different arena of imitation. Rather than mimicking a part of the insect's life cycle, these considerably larger, more flamboyant flies repre-sent small baitfish: sculpin minnows and the like.

The main difference between the two is that streamers are tied with feathers, and the bucktails, as the name implies, are tied entirely with hair. Both do the same job.

Streamer fishing requires more rod and line manipulation, in order

CAM'S HALF-DOZEN STREAMERS AND BUCKTAILS

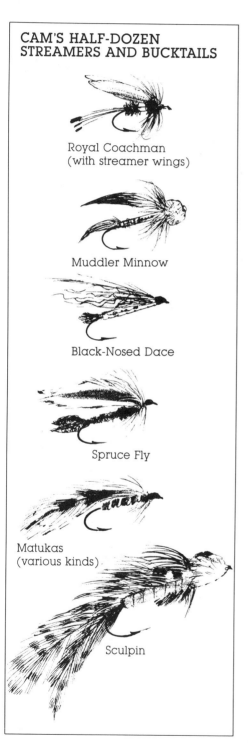

Royal Coachman
(with streamer wings)

Muddler Minnow

Black-Nosed Dace

Spruce Fly

Matukas
(various kinds)

Sculpin

to properly duplicate the motion of the tiny fish. Small, quick movements of 6 inches to a foot will represent the minnow darting about from its normal hiding place beneath rocks. Longer, smoother motions can be made to duplicate the little fish nosing about the bottom for food.

Joe Brooks's List
1. Black Ghost
2. Gray Ghost
3. York's Kennebago
4. Lady Ghost
5. Black-Nosed Dace
6. Colonel Fuller
7. Supervisor
8. Wilson's Special
9. Mickey Finn

Cam's Half-Dozen
1. Royal Coachman (with streamer wings)
2. Muddler Minnow
3. Black-Nosed Dace
4. Spruce Fly
5. Matukas (various kinds)
6. Sculpin

If you were restricted to a single fly here, it would have to be the Muddler Minnow, one of the great fishcatchers of recent years. Don Gapen tied the first one in 1948, and since then it's become a favorite of anglers from coast to coast.

FISHING STREAMERS AND BUCKTAILS
As a rule, large fish like large flies, and this accounts for the success of streamers and bucktails in taking big fish.

Breather flies—flies tied with flared wings—are common in both streamer and bucktail flies. When they are pulled through the water, the wings close. At rest, the wings flare out again. This opening-and-closing, or "breather," action gave them their name.

When fishing streamers and bucktails, it is wise to check the fly frequently. The long wings and bucktail over the back of the hook will often lay over and under the body, catching in the bend of the hook. This ruins the action and looks unnatural.

Most anglers use streamers and bucktails very effectively early in the season, in high and discolored water. However, they frequently produce well during low, clear water conditions as well.

The most productive method of fishing is the broadside float, fished across stream. Cast slightly upstream and across. Let the fly float broadside, leading the line with the rod tip. Using the strip method retrieve, strip the fly in short jerks, let it float briefly, then strip again.

If the belly of the line gets ahead of the fly, it will turn and be pulled headfirst downstream, so you should mend the line upstream. If, on the other hand, the fly gets ahead of the line, it will turn tail downstream. Mend the line downstream to turn it broadside again.

Let the fly swing in below you, and before you pick up for another cast, strip the fly a few feet to tantalize a waiting fish. When fishing the streamer or bucktail, keep the rod above and parallel to the water to absorb the shock of a strike.

Streamers are good hunting flies when there is no obvious fish activity, or you're looking for that really big fish. When fishing the streamers, be

creative. Vary the retrieve with long and short strips of the line, and make it look as much as possible like the naturals it imitates.

TERRESTRIALS

At least some portion of the fish's diet will be made up of terrestrial insects that have fallen into the water. At times when the aquatic insects are showing little or no action, a terrestrial may be just the thing.

The two most common terrestrials we imitate are the grasshopper and the ant. Unlike the old myth, there seems to be no particular merit to one over the other, except for what the fish are going for that particular day.

If there is a natural condition, say a cloud of grasshoppers swept into the water by a gust of wind, then you will naturally want to duplicate that.

Cam's Half-Dozen
1. Joe's Hopper
2. Black Ant
3. Letort Cricket
4. Ginger Ant
5. Beetle
6. Inchworm

There are a number of other useful patterns, but these are probably the strongest catchers. Again, depending on the local conditions, you

---

ANGLER'S HINT

Sparsely tied wet flies and nymphs usually produce better than full-bodied flies.

CAM'S HALF-DOZEN TERRESTRIALS

Joe's Hopper

Black Ant

Letort Cricket

Ginger Ant

Beetle

Inchworm

may have to try a size or two to get at the right combination.

Oddly enough, fish will fairly often strike an artificial fly that is slightly smaller than the naturals they are eating, so it pays to have a few of the smaller flies in your box.

SPECIAL FLIES

In addition to these basic lists, there are several patterns that deserve special comment. Some of them spread across several categories, or don't quite fit any. But they are among the most solidly proven fish getters in all kinds of circumstances.

The Muddler Minnow is one of the best fish-catching flies of all times, but nobody seems to know what it means to the fish. It is fished wet, but that's about the only consistency. Sometimes it appears to be a hopper, or a streamer, a bug, or even a small mouse. Whatever it is, it's a very good fly-of-last-resort.

Also excellent is the Dan Bailey combination of the Spruce Fly Streamer and the Muddler, called the Spuddler. It is tied with the body and head of a Muddler, with Spruce Fly wings.

The Skating Spider is another anomaly that gets fish without fitting anybody's theory. Fashions in fly fishing change rapidly, and today, almost nobody fishes the Skating Spider. You would probably have some difficulty finding them for sale. Still, such respected experts as A. J. McClane and Joe Brooks swore by them when everything else failed.

The Skating Spider is fished dry, perching as delicately on the surface

SPECIAL FLIES

Muddler Minnow

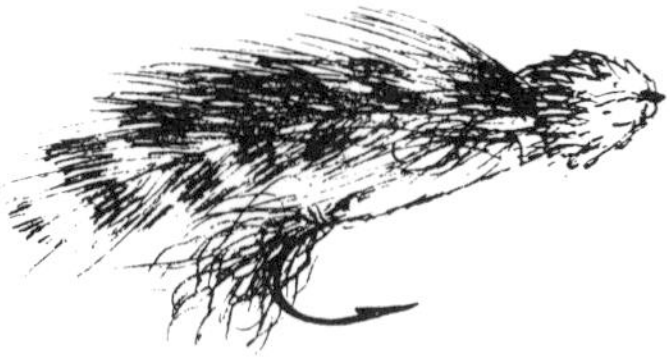

Spuddler

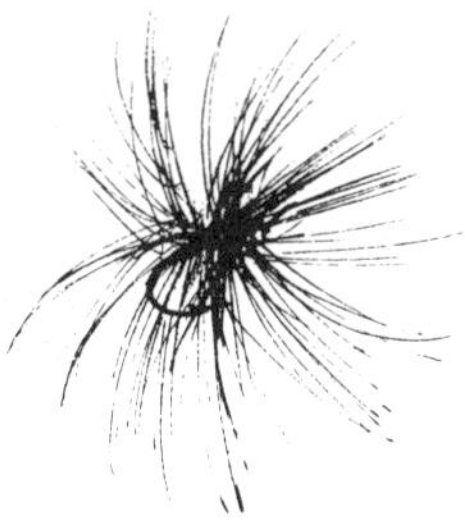

Skating Spider

Wooly Worm

Soft-Hackled
Flies

as possible. It is one of the easiest patterns to present delicately, as it is virtually just a ball of light hackles. They can be skated lightly across the surface, hence the name Skating Spider.

The Wooly Worm is fished wet. Strictly speaking, it's a terrestrial, in that it mimics the caterpillar. It, too, is an all-time high scorer in a wide variety of conditions. The orange and black pattern of the wooly bear caterpillar seems to work best, though the other colors are also effective in their place.

In recent years there has been a growing popularity of a new kind of fly entirely, called the soft hackled fly. This is a relatively new design, and is coming to have a lot of acceptance among anglers, particularly those in the Western United States.

The secret of the soft hackled fly seems to be that it does not rest *on* the surface film, but *in* it. This seems to make it very attractive to fish that are feeding on the surface.

Perhaps it implies an airborne fly without enough energy to escape. In any case, it has often been observed that a fish will take a soft hackled fly in preference to a dry fly right beside it. It's worth trying, in any case.

FLY TYING

One of the fascinations of fly fishing is the range of other knowledge it leads to. The artificial fly itself is a subject of great breadth—there is literally no end to the exploration of fly patterns and types.

Tying the artificial fly is a craft in its own right, a compelling combination of aesthetics and function which

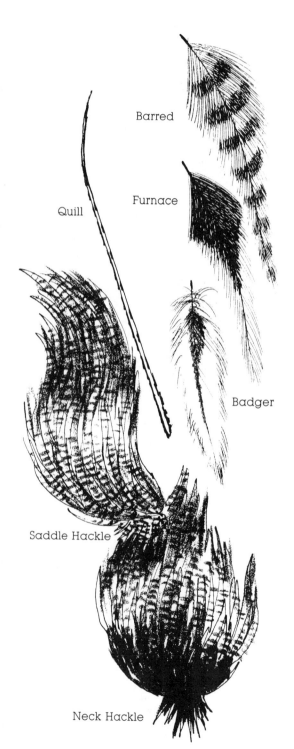

Barred

Furnace

Quill

Badger

Saddle Hackle

Neck Hackle

can provide you with endless hours of enjoyment, better fishing, and save you money in the long run.

MATERIALS

The basic materials of fly tying are feathers, fur, and hair, as they have been for two thousand years. So specialized are the requirements of the artificial fly, however, that the feathers used are from chickens raised for that purpose alone.

There have been numerous books devoted to the technique of tying your own flies. In the scope of this book, we will be able to give you enough information to know whether or not you wish to progress further, and an idea of the basic procedures.

Written instructions are no substitute for a good teacher. If you decide to try your hand at tying, you will save a great deal of time and frustration by enrolling in a fly tying class. These are available in almost every area, either through clubs or individuals. Your tackle shop will be able to steer you to a good teacher, and it is definitely recommended.

Some of the terms used in fly tying are a bit confusing, because they often refer both to the material, and the use to which it is put. A good example is the term you will find again and again, the "hackle."

Strictly speaking, a hackle is a feather, and specifically a long, narrow feather from the neck of a rooster or hen. (A saddle hackle is a feather from the *back* of the bird.)

Terms like "grizzly," "ginger," "furnace," and so forth, indicate the color and/or pattern of the hackle. Some particularly rare or valued colors can be very expensive. A first-rate natural grizzly neck (containing up to three hundred hackles) presently costs about $55. Some of the more scarce natural varieties are also simulated with color processing.

The other use of the word "hackle" refers to a specific part of the fly. The hackle of a fly refers to a feather wound around the hook shank at right angles, so that each fiber of the feather sticks out individually.

This is of particular importance in the dry fly, as it floats on the hackle. Whether it is bushy or sparse, long or short, stiff or flexible, has much to do with the appearance and the way the fly will ride on the water.

The quill of the feather also has many different uses in fly tying. Stripped of its fibers, the quill is used as a tail, or wound around the hook shank to simulate the segmented body of many insects.

FLY TYING TIP

Take care to position each addition carefully *before* you begin to tie it off. It is usually impossible to adjust it "as you go." If it is not positioned correctly at the beginning, it never will be.

"Dubbing" materials are generally animal furs, used for the body of the fly. Again, a wide variety is available, ranging through rabbit, muskrat, beaver, fox, and otter.

The parts of the artificial fly are shown in the accompanying illustration: the body, wings, tail, and hackle. (Individual legs are also sometimes simulated.)

PARTS OF A FLY

Wings

Body

Tail

Hackle

Here is a list of the materials commonly used for the different parts. Needless to say, this is a very abbreviated catalog; the ingenuity of the fly tyer knows no limits.

BODY

- Animal furs
- Wool yarns
- Synthetic yarns
- Quills
- Chenille
- Silk floss
- Tinsel

WINGS AND TAIL

- Chicken feathers
- Mallard flank feathers
- Duck quill feathers
- Bucktail and deer hair
- Marabou feathers
- Peacock herl

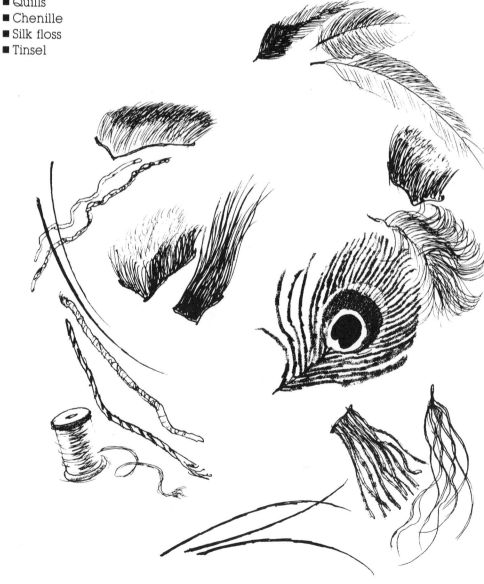

LEGS

- Animal hairs
- Feather fibers
- Small quills
- Synthetic fibers

Obviously it could be an extensive project to assemble all these materials one at a time. Fortunately, most tackle shops have kits of tying materials already put together with a good variety of materials.

PROCEDURES

The procedures given here are not for a specific pattern, but for the general type. Specifications of material and style for individual flies can be found in any of the numerous books devoted exclusively to the craft.

It is a good idea at the beginning to use a large hook, say a #2, until you are reasonably familiar with the procedures. The materials will be easier to handle, and you will be able to see what you are doing.

The Tail

1. Secure the tying thread to the hook. Holding the running end of the thread along the shank with the left hand, make a number of turns around thread and shank with the bobbin, working back from the eye. When the thread is secured, clip off loose end. Continue wrapping back to the bend of the hook. Let the bobbin hang, which keeps tension on the tying thread.
2. Fan a feather to expose the individual fibers. Tear away a segment that is made up of 12 to 18

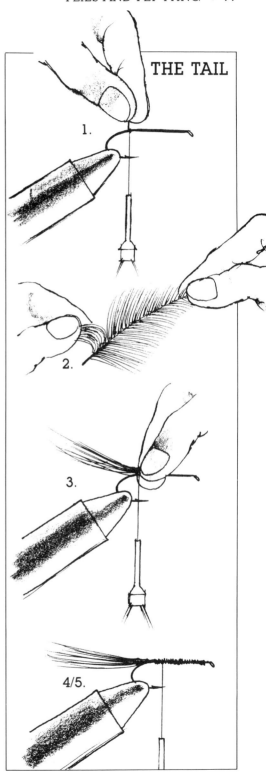

THE TAIL

1.

2.

3.

4/5.

individual fibers, keeping the ends aligned. Measure against the hook. (The tied length should be about the same as from the eye to the bend.)

3. Hold the fibers at about a 45-degree angle across the top of the shank. Take a turn with the tying thread at the beginning of the bend to secure the tail.

4. Now align the fibers straight along the shank, take a few more turns forward of the first one, and trim off the stubs. Take a few more turns to cover the ends, then wrap back to the bend.

5. The tail should now project back about the length of the shank. You may wish to dab on a bit of lacquer or head cement to secure this tie.

ANGLER'S HINT

Gold and black are good choices for fishing dark, discolored water.

The Body

6. Beginning at the bend of the hook, tie on a length of peacock herl.

7. Wind the herl forward along the shank, keeping each turn close together to form a substantial bulk. Be sure not to wind so far forward that no room is left for wings and hackle.

8. Tie off herl with a couple of turns of tying thread. The end of the herl should be on the bottom of the shank.

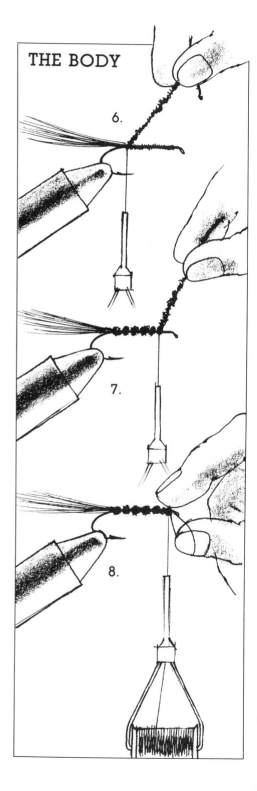

THE BODY

6.

7.

8.

The Wings

9. For the wings you will need a matched pair of primary feathers, one from the left wing and one from the right. Cut a segment from the leading edge of each feather about 3/16 inch wide.
10. Hold this pair of segments together, concave sides facing each other, tips evenly aligned. The difficult part of wing tying is holding the feathers precisely while you are tying.
11. Position the wings on top of the shank. The length should be about equal to the length of the hook, but *the wings are tied with the points facing forward.*
12. Tie in the wings with a couple of turns of tying thread.
13. Clip the stubs and wrap a "shoulder" of tying thread ahead of the wings to force them back into an upright position.
14. When the wings are standing upright, wrap a few figure-eight turns between them to separate them.

The Hackle

15. Tie in the hackle feather ahead of the wings, holding it at a 45-degree angle across the shank for the first wrap.
16. Holding the tip of the hackle in your hackle pliers, wind the rest of the length around the shank so that the individual fibers stand out and away from the shank. For a sparse hackle, one hackle feather may be enough, but for a bushier one you will use two, or even more.

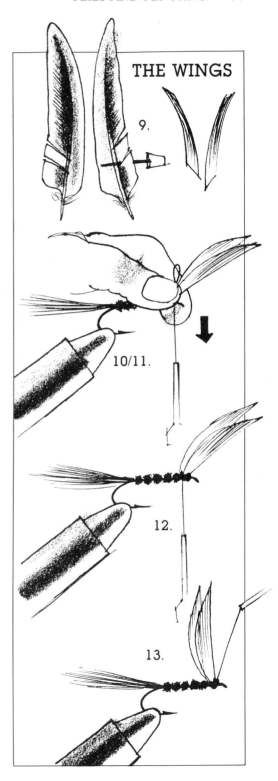

THE WINGS

9.

10/11.

12.

13.

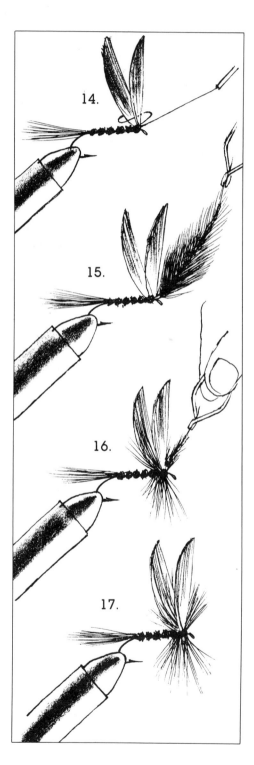

14.

15.

16.

17.

17. When completed, the wings should project slightly above the hackle.

The Whip Finish

18. Bring the tying thread up to a vertical position, and form a loop. Bring the free end horizontally along the near side of the shank, just behind the eye.
19. Keeping the loop taut, wrap it four or five times around the horizontal line to secure it to the shank. (Pass the thread back and forth between left and right hands, making sure always to maintain tension.)
20. Keep tension on the loop, draw the free end back, closing the loop and sealing the knot. Clip free end of tying thread.
21. Put a dab of head cement or clear lacquer to finish.

This is generally the pattern you will follow to tie a typical dry fly. The materials will vary from pattern to pattern, but will usually be tied on in the same way.

In the classic flies, there are several proportions that remain pretty well constant. The tail is equal to the length of the shank from just behind the eye to the beginning of the bend. The hackle is approximately the same. Wing length is slightly longer— from the eye to the farthest curve of the bend—to allow the wings to project above the hackle in the finished fly.

There are variations in proportion for streamers, bucktails, and wet flies, which would be described in a book detailing specific patterns.

Wings and tails are always tied on top of the hook, while hackle and

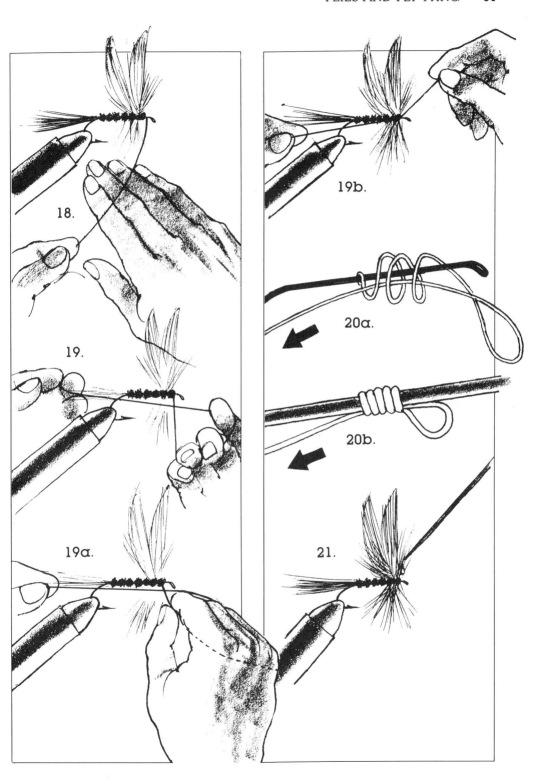

18.

19.

19a.

19b.

20a.

20b.

21.

body materials are tied in beneath the shank.

You will usually wrap over and away from you; that is, clockwise for a right-handed tyer and counterclockwise for a left-hander.

CHAPTER 6

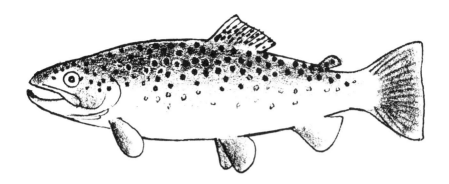

CASTING TIPS AND TECHNIQUES

FLY CASTING

The basic physical skill in fly fishing is, of course, casting. The purpose of casting is *to place the fly exactly where you want it.*

That is emphasized because beginners lose sight of it almost immediately, and even many experienced anglers behave as though they don't know it.

It is NOT the purpose of casting to throw the longest possible distance.

For some reason buried deep in the human ego, we all have the desire to cast great distances. Tournament casting, devoted to distance, is a sport which is entirely separate from that of casting for fish.

The distance mania goes to some quite absurd lengths, such as anglers who buy a 30-yard line rather than 35, in order to be able to cast *all* their line with 15 feet less effort.

But in casting for fish, it is the accuracy and delicacy of presentation that matters. There is no question that a perfect cast of 30 feet will take more fish than a sloppy one at 60 feet, however impressed your fellow anglers may be. And remember that the majority of fish taken fly casting are within about 40 feet of the angler.

When learning a new piece of music, the musician doesn't try to play it at top speed immediately. He concentrates on accuracy of the notes, and the speed follows naturally.

The same is true in learning to cast the fly. You will save yourself a great deal of frustration if you concentrate on perfecting your form, rather than trying for distance at any cost. Distance will come automatically as your form improves.

As with any physical skill, there are limits to how much a book can teach you. There is no substitute for a teacher who can correct you with every cast, and there is no substitute for steady practice. The fastest, most efficient way to learn casting is (1) to take a class from an experienced angler, and (2) to practice regularly.

And on the subject of practice: Half an hour a day for a week is a hundred times better than four hours once a week. Probably three and a half hours of that four will be spent in practicing your mistakes.

Both your physical coordination and your focused attention tend to dwindle rapidly when learning a new skill. This is a pretty fixed law of learning, and you might as well acknowledge it. Your determination to keep on going will not help. Keep your practice sessions comparatively short, but *regular*.

Also, practice is practice and fishing is fishing. If you try to practice your casting and fish at the same time, you are almost guaranteed to do a dismal job on both. When you are fishing, there are a thousand other considerations to occupy your mind. You cannot possibly devote the necessary attention to the mechanics of casting and the challenge of fishing at the same time.

With the exception of the roll cast, virtually all of your casting practice can be done on dry land. Since we are not trying for long distances at first (remember?), your back yard is probably perfectly adequate.

In fact, your first few practice sessions should be in your own living room, with only the butt of your rod— no line, no fly. The first thing you are going to do is to teach your muscles to expect a certain sequence of movements.

THE BASIC CAST

Fashions change, even in casting. A previous generation taught what might be called the "wrist-snap" technique of casting, in which the action was restricted to the forearm and wrist. It was often taught by holding a book under the arm to restrict motion.

The modern theory of casting could be called the "push-pull" school. It has been described in most detail by Doug Swisher and Carl Richards, in their book *Fly Fishing Strategy*, and uses movement of the upper arm and shoulder as well as the wrist.

The push-pull method is a better technique for several reasons. It is a more natural movement, it directs the casting force more efficiently, and it is more precisely controllable. It is superior to the old method in almost every respect. Most experienced an-

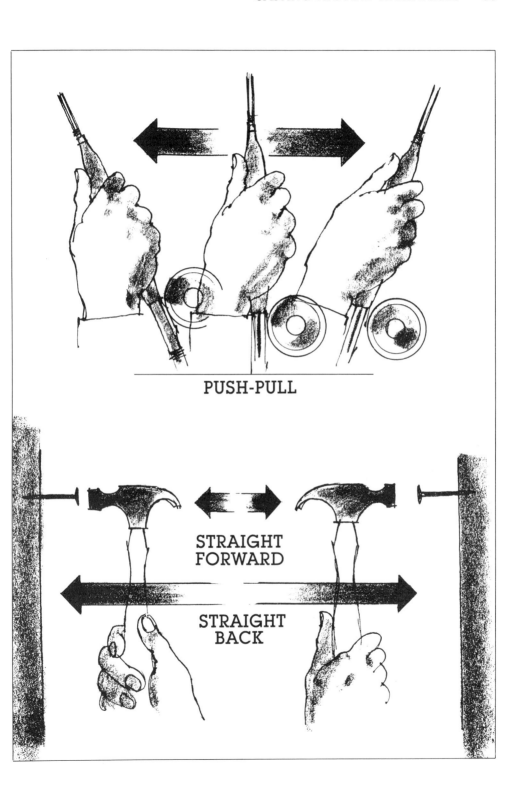

PUSH-PULL

STRAIGHT
FORWARD

STRAIGHT
BACK

glers, in fact, have *always* used this in practice, regardless of how they were taught.

The key to this method is that the rod tip is moving in a *straight line* for most of its travel, not an arc.

Think of yourself standing against a doorjamb, trying to pound a nail over your shoulder. If your wrist breaks too much, sending the hammer in an arc, you will bend the nail instantly. The movement has to be *straight* back.

Similarly, to pound a nail in the opposite jamb, the hammer has to move *straight* forward to the contact.

This "hammering" motion is a crude but fairly accurate representation of the motion of your arm in push-pull casting.

The grip you take on the rod can help you achieve the right motion. While there are several ways to hold the butt of a rod, by far the best is with the thumb on top.

Grip the rod easily, with the ball of the thumb at the front of the cork handle. As you become tense, you

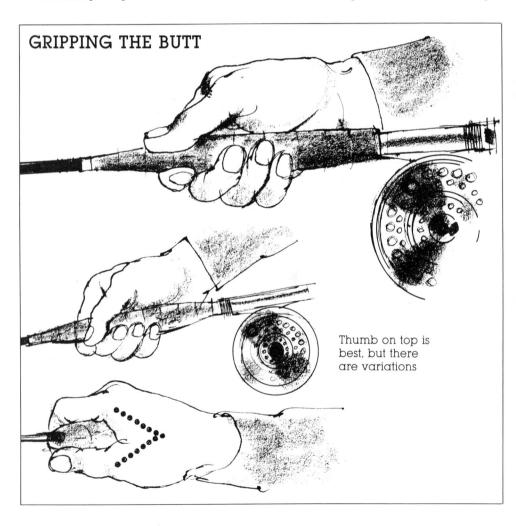

GRIPPING THE BUTT

Thumb on top is best, but there are variations

will find you tend to roll forward with the *tip* of the thumb exerting pressure. Relax. Keep pressure on with the whole ball.

This grip provides the most power, and also prevents the wrist from breaking back on the backcast, one of the most common errors.

DRY RUNS

LESSON ONE—INDOORS, NO LINE, NO FLY

It is worthwhile practicing this *straight* push-pull with just the butt of your rod, in slow motion.

1. Visually line up the tip with a ceiling edge (or other straight line). With your hand about shoulder level, and the rod vertical, *push* forward, with the tip following your reference line. *Pull* back in the same way. The rod should be kept vertical through the whole stroke.

Don't rush it. Just let your shoulder and arm muscles become familiar with the motion. Coordination and speed will come along, but first your arm has to store the "image" of that straight push-pull. Watch your rod tip and keep the movement *straight*.

2. When you have the feel of the straight push-pull with no wrist action, we can begin to bring the wrist in. At the end of the forward stroke, let the rod tip dip from vertical to about the eleven o'clock position. STOP. Look at it. Eleven o'clock is not very far off vertical.

Now, *with the rod angle still at eleven o'clock*, come back with your straight pull until your hand is about even with your shoulder. At the end of the pull stroke, let your wrist break back to incline the rod at the one

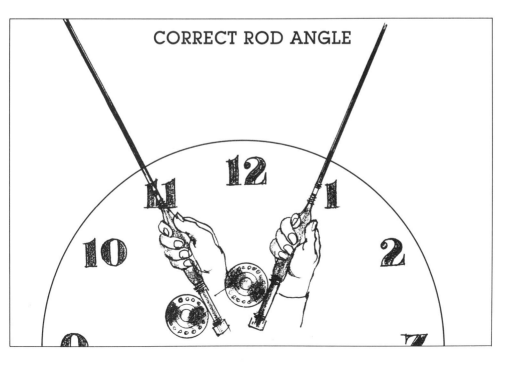

CORRECT ROD ANGLE

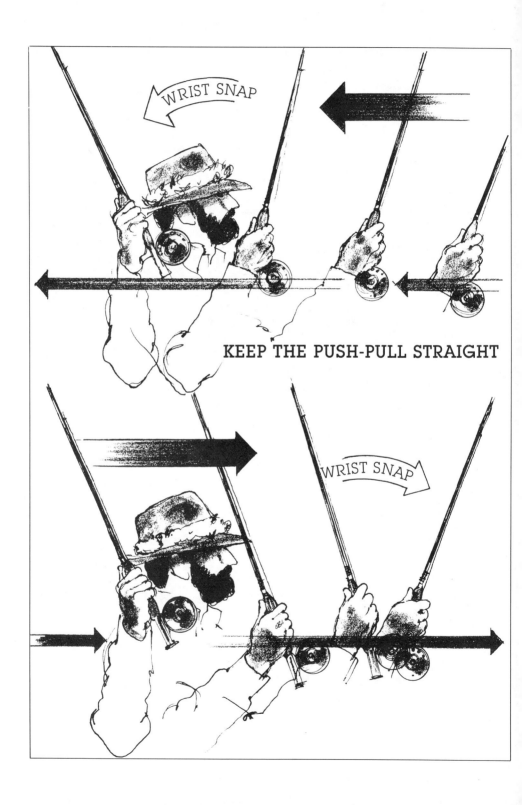

WRIST SNAP

KEEP THE PUSH-PULL STRAIGHT

WRIST SNAP

o'clock position. STOP. Look at it. One o'clock is not very far off vertical.

On the next forward stroke, the rod is *kept at the one o'clock position* through the push stroke to the end, then allowed to drop to the 11 o'clock position.

Practicing this in slow motion can save you hours in the field. The most common error of beginners is to change the rod angle at the *beginning* of the stroke, rather than the end, particularly on the backcast. Don't let your wrist cock until the end of the straight movement.

In actual practice with a line, you will impart some force with that wrist movement, but for these dry runs, just *allow* the rod tip to assume the eleven and one o'clock positions. The "snap" will come quite naturally by itself.

Now you can practice the pull-cock, push-fire movements continuously. SLOWLY. Watch your rod position attentively. You're not throwing anything, you are accustoming your muscles to a particular sequence of actions. Don't forget to STOP at the end of each stroke and observe the angle of your rod. (When you begin throwing line, this STOP period will

---

ANGLER'S HINT

Make it a habit, when fishing wet flies and nymphs, to lift the rod tip at the end of the swing and then drop the tip before beginning the retrieve. A fish will often be following the fly and the drop back will place it directly on his nose.

---

form the basis of your timing, allowing the line to straighten completely.)

The best thing about this exercise is that it will bore you rather quickly. That's great. Five minutes at a time is plenty. Quit, and daydream about the magical trout that await you far from your living room. Then practice again. It won't take long before the coordination of the movement becomes automatic.

LESSON TWO—OUTDOORS, WITH LINE, NO FLY, RIGHT HAND

When you are accustomed to combining the push-pull with the wrist action at the end of each stroke, assemble your rod with line and leader and go outside.

There is no good reason to have a hook and fly on the end of your tippet at this point. A piece of brightly colored yarn is much more practical as a practice fly, giving you good visibility and subject to many fewer tangles. Also, when it clips you behind the ear (and it will), you will find a piece of soft yarn considerably more agreeable than a number 6 hook.

For reasons of visibility, it is a good idea to have a brightly colored fly line, yellow or green, as you will be watching it a good deal. Much of your observation will be against the sky, but you will want to know precisely how your line falls on the "water."

You will find you have an uncanny natural ability to tie overhand knots in your leader while it is in midair. If you were *supposed* to do it, it would be almost impossible. However, after your first few hours, you will probably have to replace your practice leader, as you will have more knots than leader.

These so-called wind knots, you should know, have nothing whatever to do with the wind. They have to do with bad casting. Nevertheless, in the field we will doubtless continue referring to them as wind knots, to spare ourselves a certain loss of face.

1. Take a comfortable stance in the middle of your clear area. Lay out about 15 feet of line on the grass ahead of you.
2. Carefully and intentionally, take your grip on the cork, thumb on top (as above). Grasp the line beneath your forefinger on the bottom of the cork to hold it firmly. Put your left hand in your pocket or something—you will not be using it.
3. Put your rod tip in the eleven o'clock position with your arm extended in front and your hand at shoulder level. With a smooth, continuous motion, *pull* the line free of the ground.
4. WATCH the line as it travels over your shoulder and unrolls behind you. It will form a kind of J shape which rapidly straightens out.
5. At the moment the line is perfectly straight behind, PUSH your hand straight forward. (Rod is in the one o'clock position.)

It will take some practice to get this timing correct, of course. Remember the STOP portion in your first exercise—this allows the time for the line to straighten out.

KEEP YOUR EYES ON THE LINE AS IT MOVES BACK AND FORTH. In due time your muscles will tell you what is happening, but at the beginning, *use your eyes*. Watch your backcast as carefully as you watch the forward cast. This will be easier if you cast slightly across your body, say 30 degrees, rather than casting straight backward and forward.

6. At the moment the line is perfectly straight in front, PULL your hand straight back. (Rod is in the eleven o'clock position.)
7. Repeat.

This is called false casting. You use it now to practice your coordination. In the field it is used to air-dry the fly, and to feed more line into the loop (Lesson Four).

While you are practicing, you will false cast a great deal. Keeping your line in control in the air is the best possible exercise in timing. And you can't learn a thing when the line is on the ground.

However, in actual fishing, you should keep false casting to the necessary minimum. Every cast is an op-

DRY RUN PRACTICE

portunity for the fish to see you and spook.

We are looking for a loop in which the sides are parallel to each other, and parallel to the ground. For the main movement, the rod tip is moving in a straight line. Only at the very end of the stroke does it assume the angled position.

Let's analyze what is happening to the forces involved in this combined movement.

During the straight push and pull movement, the entire rod is being flexed—or "loaded"—by the weight of the line. When the wrist snaps forward or back, extra power is being delivered at the very tip. One way to look at it is that the straight movement actually propels the line, and the wrist snap at the end turns the tippet over to the full straight position.

Things to watch for:

1. Rod angle. Most beginners allow the rod tip to drop well past the one o'clock position on the backcast.
2. Rushing the backcast. Remember the definite pause that allows the line to straighten before applying forward movement.
3. Allowing the wrist to break *during* the push-pull, rather than at the end. The "snap" comes smoothly as the termination of the push-pull.

SHOOTING LINE

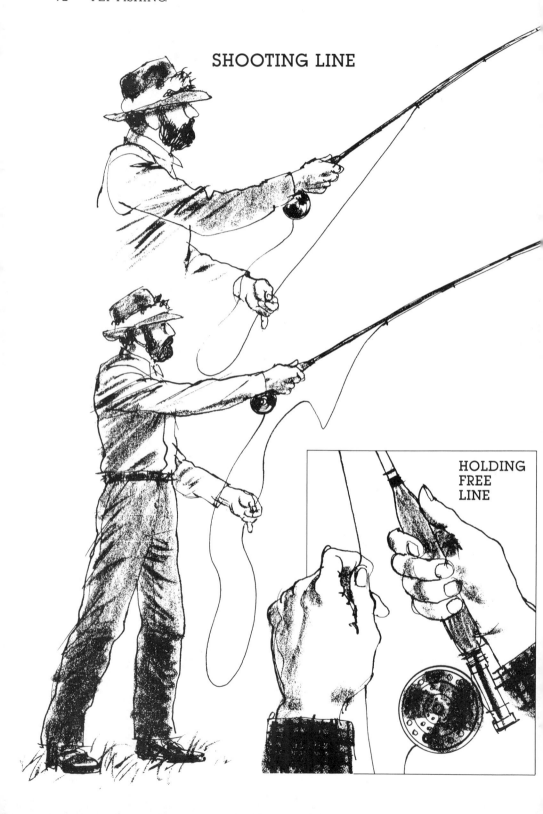

HOLDING FREE LINE

Practice false casting until you have a reasonable percentage of well-formed loops. When you have the timing correct, you will feel a consistent tension on the rod throughout the movement.

You will very often find that once you "feel" the proper timing, your second or third cast after that will be the best. Then you lose it. This happens even to experienced anglers.

LESSON THREE—OUTDOORS, LINE, NO FLY, LEFT HAND

Now you can take your left hand— your line hand—out of your pocket.

1. Grasp the line (previously held under your right forefinger) between your left thumb and forefinger. The left hand is held rather close to the rod, about the same level as your right hand. The line now runs from the stripping guide on the rod to the left hand.

2. Begin false casting again. Everything is done the same way, except now the line is held steady by the left hand, rather than against the rod.

3. As you cast, the line should be as fixed as when you were clamping it to the rod. The line hand remains at waist level.

Rod angle too low

Rushing backcast

Wrist snap during push

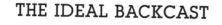

THE IDEAL BACKCAST

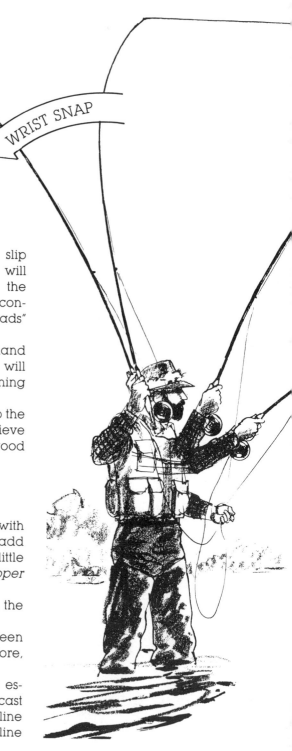

WRIST SNAP

If you allow the line to slip through your left hand, you will find you have dissipated the power of the stroke. It is the constant tension on the line that "loads" the rod.

Also, if you let your line hand wave back and forth, you will never be able to feel the timing come correctly.

4. Practice this until you can keep the line tension constant, and achieve a reasonable percentage of good loops.

LESSON FOUR—SHOOTING LINE AND TARGETING

When you are fairly consistent with the line hand, you can begin to add line to the loop by releasing a little through the line hand *at the proper time*.

1. Strip 8 or 10 feet of line from the reel and let it fall at your feet.
2. Grasp the line lightly between forefinger and thumb as before, and begin false casting.
3. When you have a good loop established, on the next forward cast release the line from your line hand, "shooting" the free line

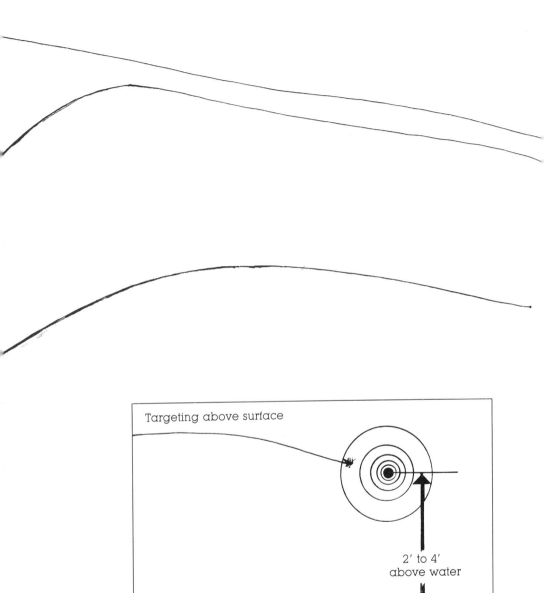

Targeting above surface

2' to 4'
above water

THE IDEAL FORECAST

WRIST SNAP

through the guides, carried by the momentum of the cast line. *This release must coincide exactly with the forward* snap of the wrist at the end of the push-pull stroke.

4. Now, *for the first time*, you may let your rod tip dip below the eleven o'clock position, to point at your target.

5. Transfer the free line to your casting hand again, holding it against the grip with your forefinger as in Lesson Two. This is the stripping position, and your forefinger is the control point for retrieving line.

   If a fish strikes at this point, all you have to do is grip the line with your forefinger and raise your rod tip to set the hook.

6. With the line still controlled by your right forefinger, use your line hand to strip a couple of feet of line back through the guides, drawing the "fly" closer to you.

7. When you have retrieved all the line you shot, make your pickup and repeat.

   If you have your false casting to a point that you don't have to think too much about it, shooting line is a relatively simple coordination, and you should pick it up quickly. If it is hard to catch, it is probably because you still have to devote too much attention to the cast itself.

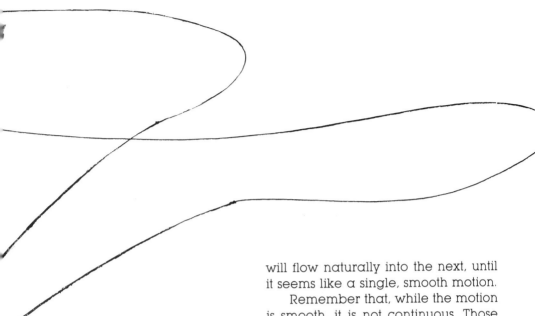

You will find the whole process easier if you don't rush it too much. Get reasonably comfortable with each step before you move to the next. Gradually it will all flow together without thought.

Targeting: Once you have adequate control over your loop, targeting is a familiar, simple procedure. You simply aim your casting hand directly at the target, as though you were throwing a ball at it.

In fishing, remember that the target is usually a point 2 to 4 feet *above* the surface. From there the fly drops lightly to the water. You do not drive the fly into the water with your cast. That's enough to frighten even the hungriest fish.

These are the fundamentals of the basic cast, step by step. With a few hours of proper practice, each step

will flow naturally into the next, until it seems like a single, smooth motion.

Remember that, while the motion is smooth, it is not continuous. Those pauses to allow the line to straighten are key elements in timing, and in getting the maximum loading of your rod for power, accuracy, and (at last) distance.

The next most important cast (some even feel it is *the* most important) is the roll cast, and that you can only do on the water. So let's find a little body of water, preferably one with no distracting fish in it, and try it.

LESSON FIVE—THE ROLL CAST
The roll cast is used to pick your line up from the water with as little disturbance as possible, and also as a fishing cast when the surroundings don't allow you enough room for a full backcast.

1. Start by false casting a few times to renew your feel of the rod, and then deliver a few casts by shooting some line. Strip retrieve as usual.

THE ROLL CAST

Picking line up from water

WRIST SNAP

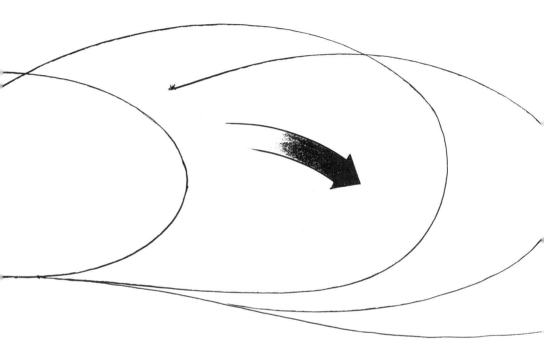

2. After a delivery cast, bring your rod up *slowly* to the one o'clock position.

3. Let your line drift back toward you until it is hanging in a slack arc just off your casting shoulder.

4. Push the rod forward, and almost simultaneously flick your wrist forward powerfully, stopping the rod at about the ten o'clock position.

Notice that the wrist action comes in more quickly than in the basic cast, and the forward angle of the rod is slightly lower.

This movement will draw the line up off the water and throw a circular loop in front of you. A properly timed roll cast will have enough force to straighten the leader out, dropping the fly in much the same way as the basic cast.

Alternatively, you can use the roll cast to begin a normal series of false casts simply by beginning your back cast at the appropriate time, rather than allowing the fly to drop to the water.

The roll cast is also sometimes useful in dislodging a fouled hook. By throwing a tight loop down the line, you can pull the hook from the opposite direction. The same technique will often turn a fish, which normally pulls against the direction of the line. These are more or less fine points, which you will get to in due time. For the moment, you will use the roll cast primarily for pickup, and for working in tighter spaces on the stream.

PRACTICAL FISHING CASTS

The basic cast and the roll cast are the fundamental skills of casting. They provide the angler with the necessary control over rod and line, and are the basis of what follows.

If you have practiced the basics until they are second nature, you will find the special casts easy to acquire.

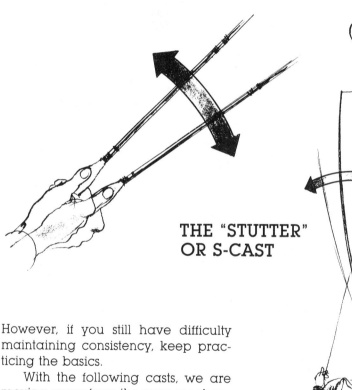

THE "STUTTER" OR S-CAST

However, if you still have difficulty maintaining consistency, keep practicing the basics.

With the following casts, we are moving away from the pure mechanics of casting, and into the area of fishing technique. These, you might say, are the actual fishing applications of what you have learned. In practice, you will probably use one or more of these special casts more often than you do the straightforward basic cast.

The S-cast: In the discussion of flies we mentioned the importance of avoiding "drag," in order to give a natural presentation of the fly. That is the purpose of the S-cast.

Drag is the condition in which the current is either retarding the line or speeding it up, thus pulling the fly through the water rather than allowing a natural float.

The principle of the S-cast is to throw a slack line, so that your line falls on the water in a series of serpentine curves. It buys you time, in effect, as the current will straighten out your slack line before it begins to drag your fly. And even a few seconds of natural float can make the difference between catching fish and not.

There are two main ways of casting the S. In the first, the delivery cast is made with a little extra force. As the forward motion completes itself, the rod is stopped quickly, and pulled back a few inches.

This causes the extending line to come to an abrupt stop, "bouncing" back in a series of curves. When you have the feel of this, you can add an extra refinement by flicking the line sharply with your line hand just as the cast reaches its full extension.

Using this method you can achieve quite a surprising amount of slack line delivered to the water, but in fishing you will want to practice a bit of moderation. If there is too much slack, you will have insufficient control over the line, and find it difficult to set the hook in the event of a strike. You will want to find a compromise between control and enough slack to minimize drag.

As your serpentine cast drifts

FISHING THE DRY FLY

The standard rule for fishing dry flies is to fish upstream. There are, as always, a number of exceptions. But it's still a pretty good practice.

It is a waste of time to cast at random across a number of fish, even when it seems they couldn't miss your fly. Each fish is in a feeding position of his own—covering a certain "territory." If you cast for a specific fish, your chances are much better.

FISHING THE WET FLY

When fishing wet flies and nymphs, remember that it takes a certain length of time for your fly to sink. You should cast *well* upstream, allowing enough time to reach the desired depth. Some nymph fishing even requires that the nymph be on the bottom of the stream, in which case it can be slightly weighted.

FISHING STREAMERS AND BUCKTAILS

Since the streamer is imitating a small baitfish, the movement you give it is very important. Short, jerky retrieves can help give the impression of a small fish darting through the water.

downstream, retrieve just fast enough to prevent the line nearest to you from being taken in the current.

The second method of casting the S is sometimes called the "stutter" cast. As your line is shooting forward on the delivery cast, you move the rod tip back and forth horizontally. Small movements are adequate; you don't want to be waving the tip all over the landscape. This will impart a series of sine waves to the line, and you will eventually be able to control the amount of slack with great accuracy.

This, incidentally, is a perfect illustration of the Number One law of casting: *Where the rod tip goes, the line goes*.

The Reach Cast: The reach cast is probably the most generally useful of the practical fishing casts. Many

CASTING TIPS

In learning to cast, concentrate on form and precision. Distance will come automatically. Long casts impress your fellow fishermen more than the fish. In addition, the more line you have out, the more difficult it is to handle efficiently. Most fish are taken relatively close to the angler.

Your local tackle shop can steer you to a class in casting. This is the quickest way to learn. A good teacher will save you many hours of practicing your own mistakes. Once you have acquired the "feel" of a proper cast, you can practice on your own.

Short, but regular, periods of practice are best. A few minutes a day in your back yard will improve your performance more than eight hours on the stream, where you have a hundred other things to think about.

The main thing to remember in the "push-pull" method is that your rod tip is moving in a *straight line* most of the time. If you swing an arc, your line will open into a loop that is too wide.

Substitute a length of soft yarn for the hook when you are beginning. It reduces tangles, hazards, and lets you concentrate on the movement of your rod tip.

A bright fly line will improve your performance in practice casting. You can't correct an error if you can't see it.

Watch your backcast as carefully as your forward cast. If your back loop is tight, your forward cast will be good.

Eventually you will know from the "feel" if your rod is properly loaded. At the beginning you will have to rely on your eyes.

CURRENT

REACH ACROSS AND DOWN

RIGHT REACH

anglers find they use some form of the reach cast on the stream more often than any other.

The object of the reach cast is to throw as much line *upstream* of the fish as possible, to allow a longer natural float. The line is cast in a wide upstream curve, so that the first thing coming down the current is the fly itself.

The first thing to do is to visualize the path you want your line to take. Then you will "draw" that line with your rod tip.

The left reach is easier for a right-handed angler. You throw your backcast in a nearly horizontal plane, with a relatively wide loop. (Don't let your loop be so wide it is uncontrollable.)

Then, as you reach forward, your casting hand sweeps down and *across the front of your body*, at about a 45-degree angle.

When you finish the cast, you will be leaning as far to the left as possible, with your rod tip nearly at water level.

Your rod tip at this point will be directed *well upstream* of the fish,

perhaps as much as 30 degrees. Your line will lie in a wide upstream curve, giving an excellent drift to your fly.

As the line begins to drift downstream, follow it with the tip of the rod. This will give you the maximum possible free float.

The right reach is accomplished by the same method, except that you will be reaching and leaning to the right. Your casting hand, of course, will go away from your body, rather than crossing it. Otherwise the same principles apply.

Casting the Curve: Casting a curve requires very precise control over your loop, and the power with which you deliver it. It is actually the

---

CASTING TIP

As with any skill, you can save yourself a lot of time by finding a teacher. A few lessons are usually well worth the trouble— and put you in touch with a lot of people who share your interests. Ask your tackle shop for names of fly tyers in your area who teach classes. Local chapters of the Federation of Fly Fishermen often sponsor classes taught by members.

THINGS TO WATCH FOR

Don't let the rod tip drop below the one o'clock position on the backcast.

Don't rush your backcast. There is a definite pause in your rod movement that allows the backcast to straighten out. If you are snapping flies off your tippet, the chances are you are rushing the backcast.

The "snap" of the wrist comes as the termination of a straight push-pull movement. Don't let the wrist break *during* the straight movement. The rod comes forward in the one o'clock angle, dropping to eleven o'clock only at the end.

CURRENT

REACH ACROSS AND DOWN

LEFT REACH

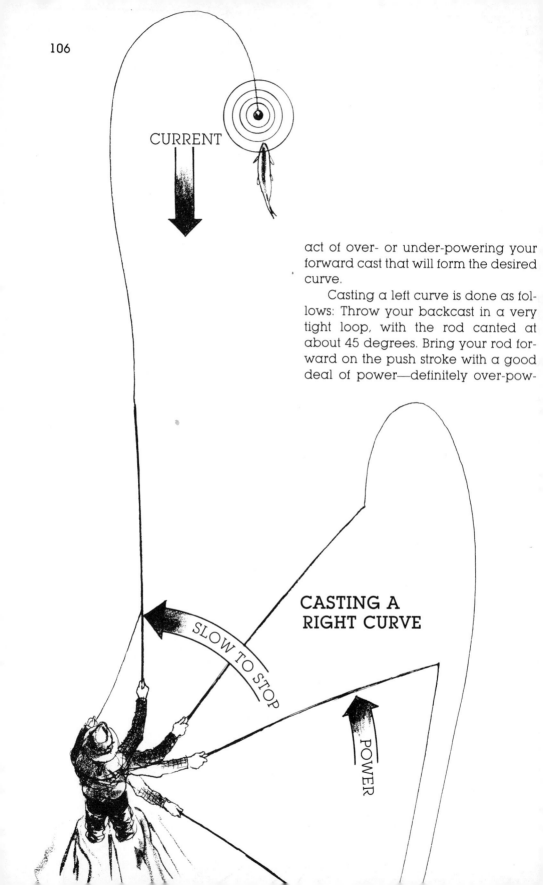

CURRENT

act of over- or under-powering your forward cast that will form the desired curve.

Casting a left curve is done as follows: Throw your backcast in a very tight loop, with the rod canted at about 45 degrees. Bring your rod forward on the push stroke with a good deal of power—definitely over-pow-

CASTING A RIGHT CURVE

SLOW TO STOP

POWER

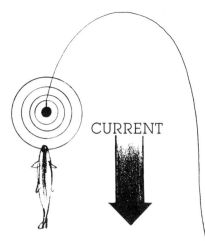

CURRENT

ered when compared to your normal cast.

This additional snap of power will not only straighten the loop but cause it to kick back, forming a "candy cane" in the other direction.

The right curve is cast with the rod almost horizontal. Here the principle is the opposite—you want to *under-power* your forward cast, so that the loop falls to the water before it has had the chance to straighten out completely.

Mastery of the curve cast will not only allow you better control of free drift but will let you present your fly in places that would otherwise be impossible. You can literally fish "around corners."

There are a great many other named casts for special situations. However, compared to the basic four, they are of very limited usefulness. The basic four will cover 99 percent of your actual fishing needs.

Everything in casting is rooted in the basic cast, and derives from it. If

CASTING A LEFT CURVE

STOP

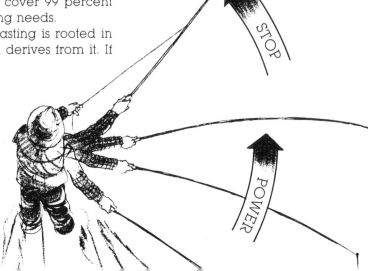

POWER

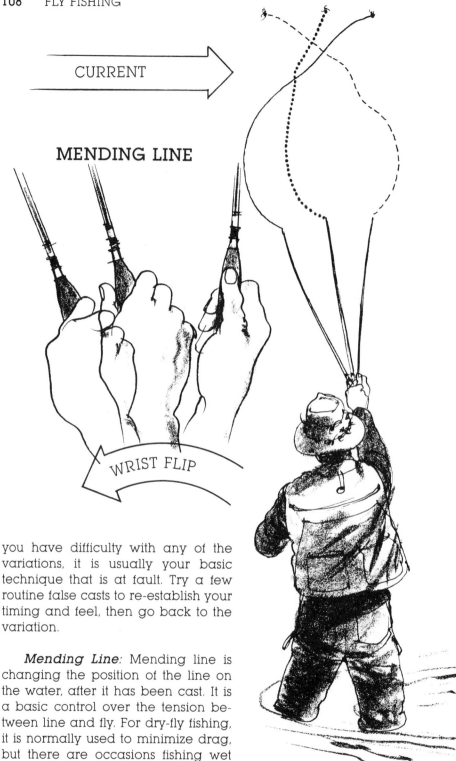

CURRENT

MENDING LINE

WRIST FLIP

you have difficulty with any of the variations, it is usually your basic technique that is at fault. Try a few routine false casts to re-establish your timing and feel, then go back to the variation.

Mending Line: Mending line is changing the position of the line on the water, after it has been cast. It is a basic control over the tension between line and fly. For dry-fly fishing, it is normally used to minimize drag, but there are occasions fishing wet flies or streamers when you deliber-

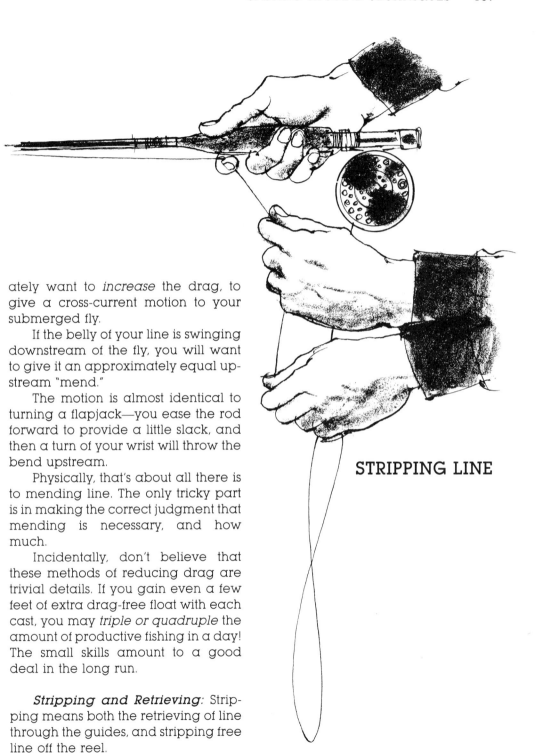

ately want to *increase* the drag, to give a cross-current motion to your submerged fly.

If the belly of your line is swinging downstream of the fly, you will want to give it an approximately equal upstream "mend."

The motion is almost identical to turning a flapjack—you ease the rod forward to provide a little slack, and then a turn of your wrist will throw the bend upstream.

Physically, that's about all there is to mending line. The only tricky part is in making the correct judgment that mending is necessary, and how much.

Incidentally, don't believe that these methods of reducing drag are trivial details. If you gain even a few feet of extra drag-free float with each cast, you may *triple or quadruple* the amount of productive fishing in a day! The small skills amount to a good deal in the long run.

STRIPPING LINE

Stripping and Retrieving: Stripping means both the retrieving of line through the guides, and stripping free line off the reel.

Remember that after the delivery

cast, you caught the free line between the rod grip and your right forefinger for control. (Many anglers use both forefinger and middle finger as their control point.)

To strip, your line hand reaches all the way up to the rod hand, and draws line back through the guides.

When fishing with streamers, which imitate minnows, a rapid strip will often impart the effect of a quickly darting baitfish. Nymphs and wet flies can also be given a convincing motion with the proper stripping rhythm. A fish that is contemplating your fly can often be coaxed into action by a sudden, escaping movement.

When imitating an escaping baitfish, your stripping rhythm may be as fast as twice a second, taking a foot or so of line with each tug. There aren't any easily stated rules for stripping speed. Your best bet (as always) is to visualize exactly what it is you

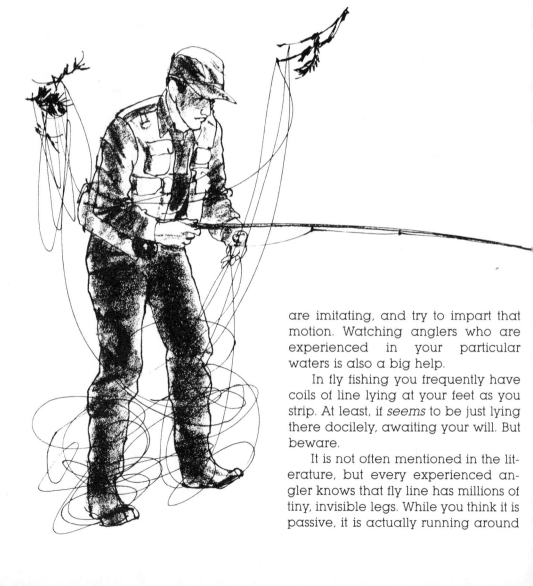

are imitating, and try to impart that motion. Watching anglers who are experienced in your particular waters is also a big help.

In fly fishing you frequently have coils of line lying at your feet as you strip. At least, it *seems* to be just lying there docilely, awaiting your will. But beware.

It is not often mentioned in the literature, but every experienced angler knows that fly line has millions of tiny, invisible legs. While you think it is passive, it is actually running around exploring every nook and cranny in the near vicinity. It is crawling under your feet and around your toes, it is wrapping itself around rocks, twigs, outboard motors, other fly rods, boxes, tying itself in underwater knots, and generally behaving like an unruly three-year-old.

All this is happening with incredible speed, but when you look down, nothing is moving. Just one more of nature's wonders.

Casting in Wind: Because the fly line is so light, it is frustratingly subject to the vagaries of the wind. And, wherever you fish, you will find very few days that are entirely wind free. It isn't really possible to practice wind corrections without wind, but if you keep a few general principles in mind, it will help.

First, the higher off the water, the stronger the wind. At 10 feet, the wind velocity may be almost double what

CASTING TIPS

Your timing depends on the "pause" that allows the line to straighten out. Without correct timing of the pause, you will never get the proper loading on your rod. You give away the spring of the rod, and might as well be fishing with a broomstick.

How well you master the practical fishing casts depends entirely on how well you have mastered the basics. If you have difficulty with the special casts, return to a straight forward cast for a few practice casts. You will usually find that you have departed from the basic principles.

At best you will probably achieve only a few yards of natural float with each cast. Every small addition will improve your chances of taking fish. It is worth working on.

In line placement, remember that the line will follow the rod tip. If the tip moves in an arc, so will the line. If the tip moves in a straight line, so will the line.

The reach cast is probably the simplest way to get as much line as possible *upstream* of the fish. With the S-cast, it is the main technique for increasing the time of natural float.

By increasing the natural float even a few feet with each cast, you may be able to get in twice as much productive fishing in the same day.

Always try to keep in mind exactly what your artificial fly is imitating. Fish are extremely sensitive to slight differences of motion. They will not strike a fly whose motion is wrong.

The main technique in compensating for wind is to keep your loops low and tight. The higher the cast, the more subject it is to the wind.

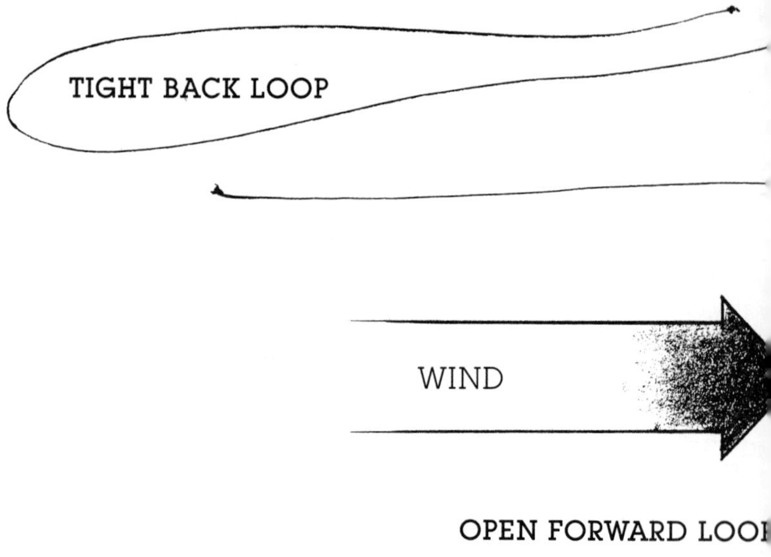

TIGHT BACK LOOP

WIND

OPEN FORWARD LOOP

ANGLER'S HINT

When fishing in cold, wet weather a good combination is a pair of light wool gloves with surgical rubber gloves over them.

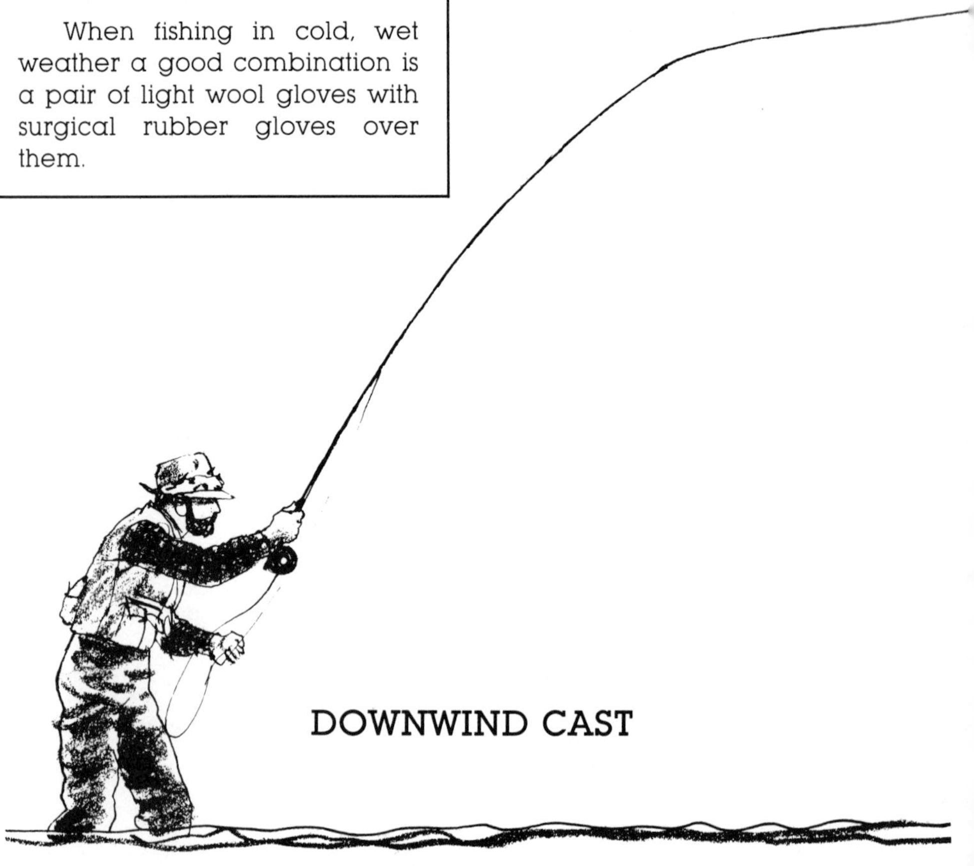

DOWNWIND CAST

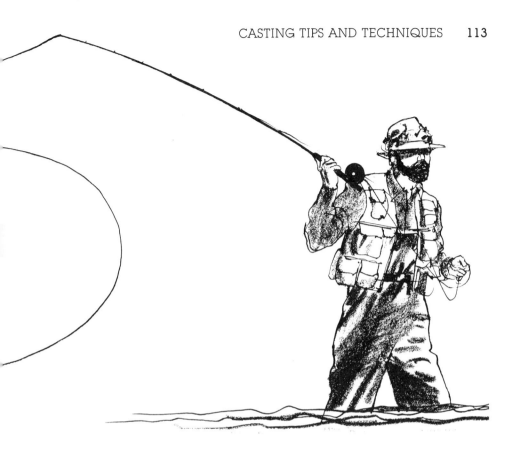

it is at 3 feet, particularly in relatively light breezes.

Secondly, the more open your loop, the more effect the wind will have on it.

The logical consequence of these two factors is that you should keep your casts low and your loops tight, particularly in the direction of the on-coming wind.

A good way of keeping your casts low is to cast side-handed, or at least at a considerable angle off the vertical.

When casting into the wind, your front loop is critical; it should be cast low and as tight as possible. The back-cast, in contrast, should be kept relatively high.

When casting downwind, the opposite is true: watch your backcast and keep it low and tight. Otherwise the wind will have a tendency to collapse the whole loop around your shoulders.

Crosswind from the left is not a great problem (for a right-handed caster.) Keep your loops tight and low, according to the general principle, and allow for windage in targeting.

ANGLER'S HINT

When stringing the rod, double the line 3 or 4 feet from the end. The loop makes it easier to string through the guides, and if it slips from your fingers it won't slip back through the guides.

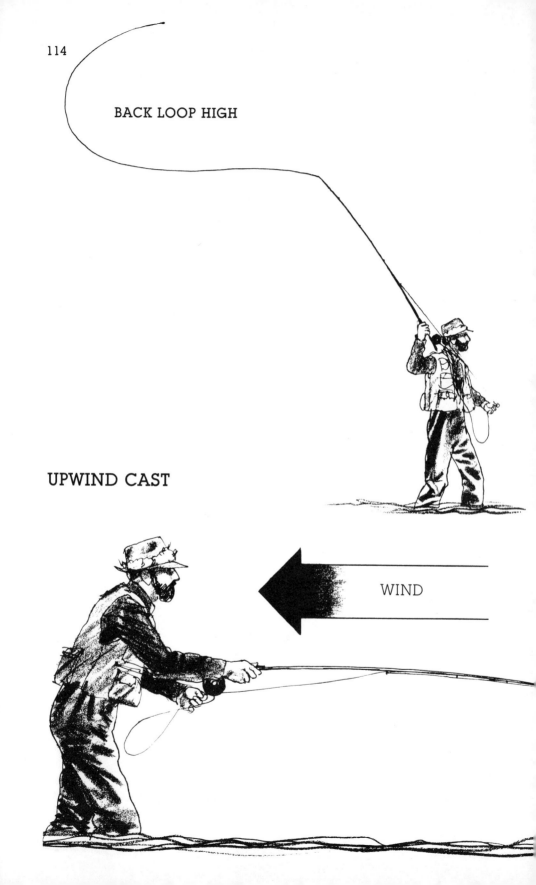

BACK LOOP HIGH

UPWIND CAST

WIND

Crosswind from the right is a more serious problem. Your hook can develop a ferocious appetite for the back of your ears. If a right crosswind becomes so strong that you cannot handle it with low, tight loops and strong delivery, the least complicated answer is to try and find a better position to work from.

There are a couple of alternatives, such as learning to cast left-handed, or delivering your forward cast over your *left* shoulder. But, generally, speaking, the beginner should try to avoid getting into competition with his own fly.

If really windy conditions are the norm for your kind of fishing, then you should consider upsizing your entire outfit to use a weight 7 or 8 line.

ANGLER'S HINT

Vary your presentation by using a dropper rig.

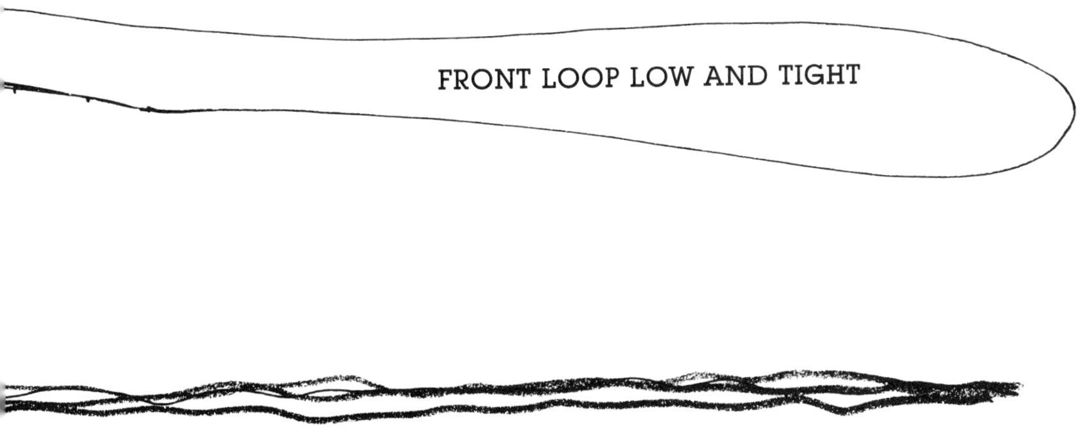

FRONT LOOP LOW AND TIGHT

CROSSWIND FROM RIGHT

WIND

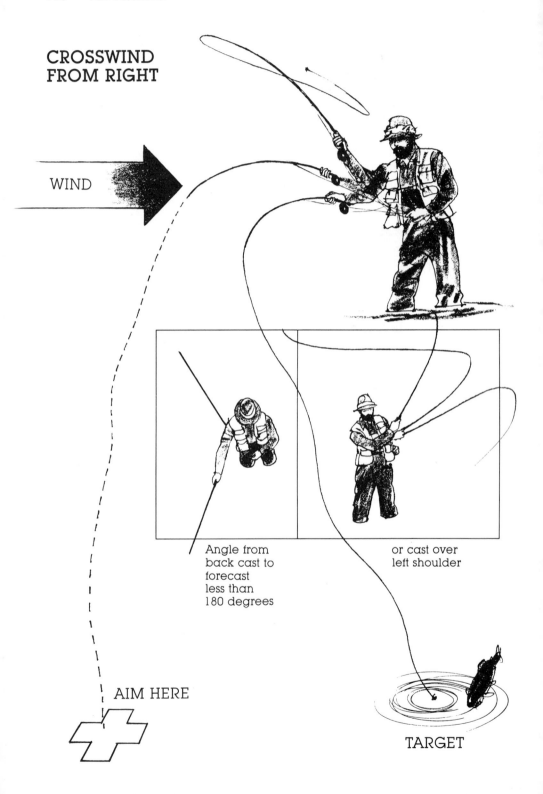

Angle from
back cast to
forecast
less than
180 degrees

or cast over
left shoulder

AIM HERE

TARGET

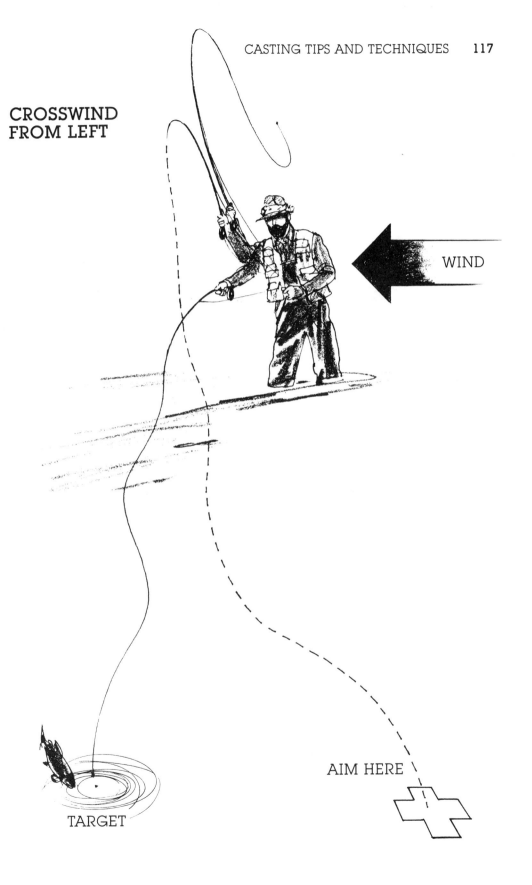

CROSSWIND FROM LEFT

WIND

AIM HERE

TARGET

CHAPTER 7

FISHING STRATEGIES

READING WATER

Reading water for fish is always some combination of previous knowledge and present observation. The proportion of each varies a great deal according to circumstance.

At one extreme, for example, is a multiple hatch of mayflies on a small Western trout stream. Here you see the fish rising to the hatch, see them take the naturals, see where they are

SEEN FROM THE BANK:
RIFFLE, RUN, POOL

in the water and how they are behaving, see the specific fish you cast
to. Everything is going on before your
eyes, and your immediate observation will be the guide. Naturally, this
will be backed up by whatever previous knowledge you can bring to
bear on the situation.

The opposite extreme might be
drifting in a small boat
on Puget Sound. You
can see no
evidence of

surface feeding,
no baitfish activity,
no bird clusters. Your tactics will be
dictated almost entirely by your previous knowledge. In this case, observation is the back-up.

However, the faculty of observation is not one that is encouraged in
our society. We are, in fact, more accustomed to turning *off* our power of
observation.

We mention this because it is the
source of a phenomenon you will notice almost immediately in the field.

*The novice does not see what is
going on around him, and he does
not know that he does not see.*

SEEN FROM ABOVE:
RIFFLE, RUN, POOL

a novice is to learn to observe, carefully and attentively. This can be summed up as Cam's Golden Rule: ***WATCH THE WATER!*** That is where the fish are. They are not on your reel, or in your tackle box, or in the clouds, or

This is not stupidity, or any personal defect. It is simply part and parcel of being a novice. At anything.

So the fastest way to cease being

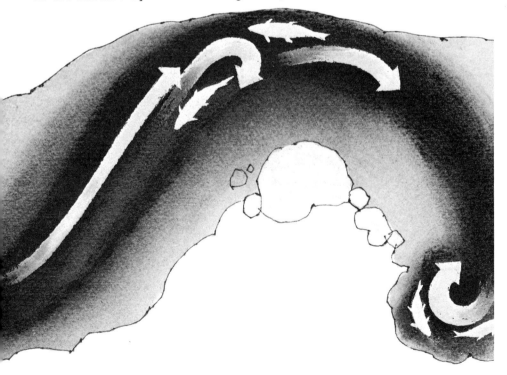

in the bottom of your boat. They are in the water, and that is where you should be directing your attention.

Incidentally, a psychologist would tell you that this careful attention is one of the major reasons fishing is such a pleasurable activity for us. For good or ill, most of us live in a world where we are always dealing with abstract things. We deal with the consequences of what we did yesterday and the plans we have for tomorrow. Today is too often no more than a harried transition between yesterday and tomorrow.

But when you are on the water, today is today, complete in itself, and that is unquestionably the reason it makes us feel peaceful. We can open up our senses and our minds freely.

If watching the water is the key to the observation side of your fishing, there is also a key to the knowledge side. This is a rather obvious principle of nature, but if you keep it firmly in mind, you will find it useful. It can clarify some otherwise quite mysterious things that fish do.

Fish are always trying to get the most possible food with the least possible effort. This principle will tell you where the fish are likely to be, and why.

So, keeping these two general principles in mind, let's look at a few different types of water, and see how they apply.

SMALL STREAMS AND RIVERS

Water naturally flowing between banks creates an absolutely characteristic bottom pattern, a kind of cycle that is repeated over and over again throughout the length of the stream. It consists of three parts: The riffle, the run, and the pool. You can look at it as the life cycle of the stream itself.

This pattern is so pervasive that you may even estimate with confidence that a natural stream will repeat it approximately every seven stream widths. That is, on a stream 30 feet wide, you will probably find a riffle/run/pool pattern repeated about every 200 feet or so.

The riffle is dancing water; the shallowest, fastest-moving portion. It is usually less than 2 feet deep, with a bottom of stones, boulder, or gravel. In extremes it may even be a small cascade, and on larger streams it is the riffle that becomes whitewater rapids.

The turbulence of the riffle digs into the bottom on the downstream side, carving out a somewhat deeper channel—the run. As the channel deepens, the current naturally slows down, and on a comparatively slow stream it also widens. This is the pool. On a slow-moving stream, the pool is considerably wider than the riffle/run portion, but on very fast streams it is a little more difficult to identify.

In the pool, the current has slowed enough that it can no longer hold the sediment it carries, and it begins to deposit it on the bottom. As the sediment builds up, the water becomes shallower and faster, leading to the formation of a new riffle, which then begins to dig a new run. And so on, and so on.

This is an ideal pattern, of course, and it is modified in a thousand ways on any real stream. Still, it is the general pattern you may expect to find underlying all the specific details.

The place a fish feeds is usually a trade-off between the amount of food

Big brown trout lay in close to the bank, out of the main current. Cast right up against the banks and overhangs.

coming down the current, and the availability of good cover. Different fish are partial to different portions of this cycle.

Riffles are (usually) too shallow to provide enough cover for large fish, and you will generally find them inhabited by minnows, baitfish, and smaller game fish. However, when a riffle is hot, it's hot, and particularly for trout. When there is a good hatch on, or a lot of nymphs, the amount of food overbalances the amount of effort required to feed in the riffle. On occasions like that, fishing the riffle can be hugely productive.

Largemouth bass, crappies, and walleyes are what might be called "pool fish," and spend the bulk of their time in the deeper waters. Surface feeding usually takes place in the "head" portion of the pool—approxi-

mately, the upper third. On hot, bright days, the same fish will probably be feeding in the deepest, stillest portion.

Trout and smallmouth bass will often hang out in the run portion. The current is still swift enough to bring a substantial amount of food to them, but it is easier to maintain position than the riffle, and the deep water is available for resting.

Yet another characteristic of streams that is important to the angler is the way in which they behave around corners.

The outside bend of a stream has the deepest water and the fastest current. The current frequently undercuts the outside bank, leaving an overhanging shelf that provides both excellent cover and a good food supply. The sediment is deposited on the inside curve, creating shallows and gravel bars. Eddies on the downstream side of bars are good places for fish to rest, but they are probably not actively feeding there.

The ideal spot for a fish is at the break between a fast current and a slow one. He can dart quickly into the faster current to feed, and then return to the slower one to rest. If the slow current also provides good shelter, so much the better.

Obstructions in the stream—logs, boulders, snags—are constantly cre-

<table><tr><td>

ANGLER'S HINT

Fish areas where springs and small stream mouths run into major rivers and streams.
</td></tr></table>

ating margins of slow and fast current, usually combined with good shelter.

Eddies behind obstructions frequently form relatively deep pools that may be good holding places for fish. The downstream side of a rocky point, for example, is a good bet.

Here are just a few of the classic holding places in the small stream or river:

1. Under overhanging banks
2. In shaded water (overhanging grass or trees)
3. In the eddies behind obstructions
4. Below islands
5. At entrances to side streams
6. Alongside and just downstream of logs.

LARGE RIVERS

It is difficult to provide a similar anatomy of large rivers in the United

States. The eastern two-thirds of the country has numerous large, warmwater rivers, but virtually none have been left in their natural state. Almost all have been dammed, diverted, polluted, and otherwise mangled beyond recognition.

In most of the country, the naturally flowing large river is a thing of the past. What once was a flowing body of water now usually takes the form of a series of long pools separated by dams. In determining your fishing strategy, you will more often be dealing with manmade characteristics than natural ones.

You may, however, apply the same general principles in analyzing a large river as a small stream—that is, look for current breaks, eddies, sheltered places, and so forth.

The man-altered river provides a number of different habitats for fish. Damming a river creates a series of different environments that are as characteristic as the natural ones. For example, almost every dammed river has a series of backwater lakes, connected to the main channel through sloughs or side channels.

THE MAIN CHANNEL

The main channel of an altered river is not usually a good fishing bet. The current is swift, the bottom usually silt or sand, with little vegetation or cover for the fish.

THE CHANNEL BORDER

This is a much more hospitable environment than the main channel. Look for obstructions like current-diverting wingdams, downed trees. Riprap shores are also good possible fishing areas.

TAILRACES

Just below the spillway of a dam is an area of turbulent water called the "tailrace." Frequently the bottom here is gravel or rock, and many of the natural conditions of shallow, swift-moving water are duplicated. In the tailrace you will find eddies (at the channel margin), backwater pools, and a variety of other conditions hospitable to fish.

LAKES

Lakes are classified by scientists on the basis of their fertility—that is, the amount of nutrients in the water from the surrounding land.

The "infertile" lakes are usually found in rocky terrain, some at high altitudes, with cold water. Many of them are in the geological area called the Canadian Shield, a huge rock-bound area that covers eastern

Dam tailraces are good holding places

BACKWATER SLOUGHS AND LAKES

During normal water levels, these areas have little or no current. There is often heavy weed growth at the edges, making good cover for large-mouth bass, crappies, and bluegills.

Other good spots on larger rivers are the mouths of tributary streams, and areas in which the water is a little warmer than average—the heated discharge from power plants, for example, often attracts a good variety of fish.

Canada and dips down into the northern United States from Maine to Minnesota. High altitude western lakes are also usually in this category.

They are generally populated by cold water species like trout, in comparatively small numbers. The relative shortage of food makes for slow-growing, slow-maturing fish.

This is one of the most fragile fishing environments, and can be rapidly overfished. In waters like these, it is almost obligatory to practice catch-

and-release. Such waters will not withstand heavy fishing pressure.

Moderately fertile lakes are found almost everywhere on the continent. They support fair-sized populations of coolwater and warmwater fish, and are not as ecologically fragile as the infertile lakes of the north.

The highly fertile lakes of the southern part of the U.S. provide some of the richest fishing ground on the continent. They are often characterized by heavy algae growths, muddy bottoms, and a profusion of weeds and other vegetation.

The fertile lakes, in later stages of their development, become warm-water marshes, particularly in the South. Fish are plentiful—largemouth bass and panfish abound.

CHOOSING YOUR FISHING STRATEGY

Your fishing strategy will naturally depend on the kind of fish, the kind of water, and the kind of fly. There is very little resemblance between dry-fly fishing on a clear mountain stream and bass-bug fishing in a more or less turbid lake.

READING WATER

Watch for drift lines that indicate the edge between a slow-moving current and a quick one. They are always likely spots, as the fish will shelter in the slow current and feed at the edge of the quick one.

Your fishing strategy will be different depending on whether you can see what's happening, or are fishing "blind." Even when fishing blind, do not assume the fish can't see *you*.

Concealment begins *before* you are in position to cast. When approaching the stream, be alert for opportunities to conceal your approach. It is sometimes even advisable to cast from *behind* a bush or rock, if the fish are particularly spooky.

When a fish spooks, you may be assured that it is something *you* have done.

Take enough time to plan your approach to the water. Study the stream before you wade out to cast. Many an eager angler has stepped right into a pool of fish feeding near the bank, spooking them irrevocably.

Work the water close to you at first, then extend your range. If you start with long casts and move in, the chances are you will simply frighten every fish in the stream with your line. Work the near side first.

A quick strike is essential. The fish knows instantly that the fly he has taken is not food, and will spit it out. Setting the hook quickly will improve your percentage of fish taken.

Generally, however, you can think of strategies in two categories: strategies where you can *see* what's happening, and strategies for fishing "blind."

FISHING THE RISE

Trout fishing during a hatch is the classic example of the first kind.

Lake fish are not on feeding stations like stream fish. They are "cruising" for food, and you must anticipate their movement, both the direction and speed.

You must keep your line taut enough not to allow the fish to throw the hook—but loose enough not to put too much pressure on him. He is reacting against your line pressure. Keep the pressure on, but gently.

Always bring the fish as close as possible before trying to land him, either by net or hand. The more line you have out, the more advantage the fish has.

The practice of catch-and-release is becoming virtually necessary if our sport is to continue. Learn to release a fish *undamaged*. It is a hypocritical gesture to release a fish that has been badly hurt in landing.

There are times during a rich hatch of mayflies when there are so many trout rising to take the naturals that a condition much like "buck fever" takes over the novice. In the excitement of the moment, you will have a tendency to cast into the general group of fish.

From the angler's vantage point, it looks as though the trout are snapping up *anything* that comes along.

However, it almost *never* works that way. Rule number one, then, is: *Pick your fish!*

Your cast should be delivered to a specific individual. As in duck hunting, shooting into a flock rarely produces any good result.

When you have determined your target, the fly should be presented directly upstream and allowed to float naturally across the fish's window of vision.

This is more easily said than done. Effective technique is a matter of avoiding mistakes as much as developing skills; and it is probably most important for you to be aware of the pitfalls.

There are several very common faults, and the novice is almost certain to make at least one of them.

GAUGING THE PLACEMENT

As you pick the fish to cast to, you will be watching the concentric circles made when he broke the surface. Remember that *the circles are floating downstream with the speed of the current.*

A common failing among beginners is to cast just above the circles—which usually presents the fly a few yards behind the fish. The fish is holding quite steadily in his place, and is usually farther upstream than you guess.

You can orient yourself by taking a bearing on some fixed point on the opposite bank—a tree, snag, rock, or whatever. You will be surprised to find how deceptive the floating rings really are.

The ideal cast is one that places the fly exactly where the fish would expect it to be, reveals only the smallest portion of the leader, none of the fly line, and above all, *none of the angler!*

majority of spooked fish have been frightened by something the angler has done. Your goal is to be invisible in the natural world, with all that implies. Here are a few hints.

Since the fish is facing upstream, the ideal is to approach from well behind. Conditions don't always allow an approach that keeps you out of the fish's window, but it is the ideal to try for.

Stealth is your best tactic. If you can do it, cast from some position where the fish can't see you at all. This

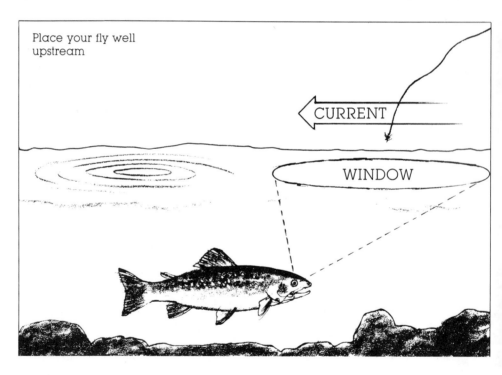

Place your fly well upstream

CURRENT

WINDOW

While it may seem to you that the fish are somewhat frenzied in their feeding—they're watching for danger as well. Rule number two is: *Stay out of sight!*

CONCEALMENT

It cannot be overemphasized that the

can mean creeping up to streamside, hiding behind foliage, trying to keep something *between* you and the fish.

Stay low; this is particularly important when approaching from the side. The closer to the fish, the lower you must be.

Keep your false casting down to

the minimum. Every movement of your rod is an opportunity for the quarry to spot you. If possible, strip enough line out of the reel to complete your delivery cast with a single false cast.

Avoid noisy wading; the sound of rocks clicking together beneath the surface travels an amazing distance.

Watch shadows; fish are very sensitive to changes of light. If you cast your own shadow, or disturb the natural shadows of overhanging trees, the chances are the fish will perceive

motion on the surface is also a common error in the heat of the moment.

MATCHING THE HATCH

If you are imitating the natural hatch with your artificial fly, *you must take the time and attention to do it.*

During a hatch, the naturals are present in several different stages simultaneously. In order to match the hatch, you *must first determine what the fish are eating.*

They may be taking the nymphs as they swim to the surface; they may

it. Be attentive to where the light is coming from.

A sloppy cast is an excellent way to spook fish. If your forward loop is too low, "driving" your fly to the surface of the water, your chances for success are low.

An inept pickup that causes com-

be taking emergers as they struggle out of the nymphal shell; they may be taking the duns as they flutter on the surface. It is not always easy to tell, but the wrong guess will guarantee you a frustrating time. Nothing is more bewildering than seeing fish rising all around, and utterly ignoring your fly.

The easiest way to tell is to ask the fish. Unfortunately, this can only be done when you are intending to keep the fish for eating. Once one has been caught, open the stomach and observe its contents directly. Note not only the insect phase but the size. Then duplicate it as nearly as your fly box will allow.

The catch here, of course, is that you have to land a fish first, in which case you will be inclined to go on fishing the same way you caught that one. Nevertheless, it is worth the trouble, and can make the difference between one lucky catch and a whole successful day on the stream.

If you can't land that first fish, pass a net through the water close to you, and examine the catch closely. You will more than likely find a selection of all the stages—nymphs, emergers, "stillborn duns" still caught in the shell, and freed duns. If the fish are feeding all around you, you won't want to do this—but it is essential.

Often the duplication of the insect species is not enough—size is very important. If the hatch that is going on consists of approximately size 16 insects, the chances are strong that size 12 hooks won't do you any good. When in doubt—*try a smaller fly.*

The usual logic is that a bigger fish wants a bigger meal, and most of the time this approach makes sense. However, there are exceptions, and if you can spot the right situation you will increase your catch by using smaller flies.

Remember the principle that the fish is trying to take in the maximum food with the minimum expenditure of energy. There are circumstances in which it will be more efficient to take

in a large number of small, easily available morsels than to use energy in moving around for the larger ones.

The fish has no efficiency experts to tell him which to do, but a few million years of evolution have honed his instincts pretty finely. The species has survived because it was *efficient.*

If the hatch goes on for some time, you may find the fish changing their tactics, and you must change yours accordingly. At the beginning of a hatch, you may find the fish's stomach has primarily nymphs, while at a later stage he may be feeding on duns.

REDUCING DRAG

Watch your fly carefully for any sign of unnatural motion—a movement across current, a tiny wake—that would indicate drag. There are times when you will intentionally *use* drag, but in dry-fly fishing the usual goal is to eliminate it entirely.

Between you and the position of your fly there are different segments of the current moving at different speeds. This is indicated by the bends and bows in your floating line. Be alert to mend line at any time the line seems to be advancing too quickly ahead of the fly, or lagging too far behind.

Mending should be as delicate as you can make it. If you splash the line off the water and splash it back on, you will have defeated the purpose.

The chances are good that even with considerable care you will not get much more than a few yards of drag-free drift. Pick up and cast again, always with the minimum possible amount of disturbance.

This is a place where short casts may work a great deal more effectively than long ones. The shorter cast is easier to deliver with delicacy, and you will get more of them per hour of fishing.

Get as close to the fish as possible, and work the nearest fish. The more chances you have for presenting your fly, the more fish you will catch.

"BLIND" FISHING

The drama of the hatch is short-lived, like the fragile insects themselves. It may last anywhere from twenty minutes to a couple of hours. In exceptional circumstances, particularly in the West, a multiple hatch of several varieties of insect may go on all day.

However, this is rare. More often you will be fishing a stream where no surface feeding is evident, and you will have to rely on your own fish-sense to find the fish. A dry fly can still produce results, but you will have to be more patient in "exploring" likely holding places. If there is no evident insect life to match, the "attractor" variety of fly—a spider, say—may be a good bet.

There is a natural tendency for the novice to become careless about concealment when he can't actually see the fish he is working. Bear in mind that all the same cautions about concealment hold whether or not you can see the quarry—a minimum of false casts, careful wading, etc.

Rather than walking up to the water and making a cast immediately, take a bit of time to study the stream consciously. Some forethought will always pay off in the end.

Go over in your mind the likely places for fish to be holding—under banks, in eddies, and so forth—and make a plan of action rather than just casting randomly. The most likely result of throwing your fly at random will be to spook any fish around. You should apply the same standard of accuracy to blind casting as when you can see your target fish.

The logical place to begin fishing a pool is at the tail, where the water begins to shallow. If you approach from downstream, you can usually move up the pool without frightening any fish that might by lying upstream.

Begin with short casts, exploring the water near you before moving out. Your first cast should be nearly directly upstream from you, perhaps 30 feet or so. As the line floats down toward you, strip in fast enough that you take up the slack, but not fast enough to cause drag.

The next cast can be made about 2 feet farther out into the stream. You continue to work a little farther out with each cast until you have either spanned the stream, or reached the end of your *accurate* casting distance. (This is usually quite some distance before your maximum.)

When you have "scanned" the tail of the pool, move upstream to a point just below where your previous casts were placed, and continue.

This systematic search of the water will give you the maximum chance of catching fish. It is a game of patience and tactics. You will find

---

ANGLER'S HINT

To fish a fly down deep, use a split shot up against the eye of the hook.

the ability to cast accurately is much more effective than long-distance casting.

If the day is bright, be especially careful to explore shaded areas under overhanging trees, grasses, and the like. On a hot, sunny day, the fish will either be holding in shadowy portions of the pool, or holding deeper.

When fishing around obstructions, remember that a fish will usually prefer to hold along an obstruction that is *parallel* to the current, rather than directly across it. A minimum of effort will allow him to dart out to get a tasty morsel and return to his shelter.

While a dry fly is possible, you will probably have better luck blind fishing with below-surface flies—nymphs, wet flies, and streamers.

A simple seine made of wire mesh between two wooden handles can be a big help in determining the kind of nymph present in the stream. By placing the seine downstream and dis-

> **ANGLER'S HINT**
>
> Carry a fly swatter for collecting grasshoppers. Float the naturals downstream first to see if fish are feeding on hoppers.

lodging the bottom with your feet, you should pick up representative examples of the nymph population, which you then match as closely as possible.

At the same time, if your seining turns up no nymphs at all, or very few, you are better advised to turn to the oldest of all techniques, the wet fly.

In either case you can use the

> **ANGLER'S HINT**
>
> A small aquarium net is handy for collecting insects on the water surface.

A simple seine of wire mesh will tell you what nymphs are present

CURRENT

same quartering technique described above for dry-fly exploration, but you will be fishing below the surface.

Nymphs and wet flies can be fished productively using across-stream casts. Sometimes you will want to allow the fly a dead drift, as in the classic dry-fly technique, but sometimes you will impart a definite motion.

Often it is helpful to mix techniques, allowing a dead drift for a while, then stripping in with short, quick motions in order to draw the fly across the current with small darting motions.

When fish are not actively feeding, it is still sometimes possible to entice them out of their holding places. One technique is called "manufacturing a hatch." This consists of dropping a dry fly in exactly the same place with repeated casts, the theory being that the repetition convinces the fish there is a small hatch on.

Another method uses streamers or some baitfish-imitating fly like a Muddler Minnow. Even if a fish is not on his active feeding station, he can sometimes not resist the substantial free meal of a tiny minnow properly placed and properly moved.

In imitating the minnow, proper action becomes very important. The quick movement of an escaping baitfish can be imparted to your fly with a combination of quick strip retrieves, a little dead drift, and twitches of the rod tip.

It can be helpful to practice this movement a little by taking a position well above clear water, where you can see the motion as you retrieve your fly. This tends to compensate for

the fact that in actual below-surface fishing, you can't really see what is happening.

LAKE FISHING

In fishing a lake, your quarry does not have the same kind of feeding station as on a moving stream. On the stream, the fish essentially maintains his own position against the flow, letting the current bring the food to him. But in a lake, the fish is cruising to *find* food.

So your main tactical problem is not to determine where the fish may be holding, but to determine in which direction and how fast he is moving.

If there is visible surface feeding, you can sometimes track the movement of a fish by the circles as he rises close to the surface. The surface insects on which a lake trout feeds are usually smaller than those on a swift stream, down to midge size.

If there is no surface feeding, it is probably a waste of time to search with a dry fly, even an attractor. The fish are most likely well below the surface.

Determining the depth to fish a lake is not always easy, but the fly fisherman can use an old trick known to bass fisherman all over the country.

Bass fishermen will tell you that light intensity is more important than temperature levels to lake fish. If you lower a white plate over the side of your boat, the depth at which it disappears is one-half the depth at which the fish are likely to be cruising. That is, if you lose sight of the plate at 10 feet, your fishing depth should be around 20 feet.

This test has the advantage that it automatically takes into account the murkiness of the water as well as the intensity of light. In early morning and evening, when the sun's rays are more inclined, the fish will tend to feed in shallower depths.

If you are going to spend considerable time on lakes, you will need a few varieties of sinking line to work with (see Chapter Three). Your casts will generally be longer, and a #7 line (with well-matched rod) is about right for most conditions.

A lake is a difficult fishing ground to approach without prior knowledge. In some lakes game fish will feed primarily on baitfish, in others there will be freshwater shrimp populations, or mayfly hatches. If you are going to fish a strange lake, take the time to talk to the local tackle shop for advice.

For fly fishing, the shallower waters around the edge of the lake are the best grounds. The kind of organisms our flies imitate can't live in very deep water. Probably the best areas (there are always exceptions) are around the mouths of streams entering the lake. These will usually produce a reasonable concentration of fish feeding on material brought in by the stream.

Other potentially productive spots are:
1. islands
2. long-submerged points
3. outlets
4. springs
5. debris near shore (logs, brush piles, etc.)
6. drop offs

Near the shores of a lake it is worth trying a terrestrial fly (say, Joe's Hopper or a Wooly Worm), as well as your normal streamers.

Without local advice, it is going to take you considerable time to get acquainted with the features of a lake and the habits of its fish; a "research" trip to the local tackle shop will be well worth your time.

PLAYING, LANDING, AND RELEASING THE FISH

THE STRIKE

The word "strike" means two different things to the angler. The first "strike" is when the fish takes your fly; the second is when you set the hook.

The strike of the fish is easiest to detect in dry-fly fishing, where the whole event takes place before your eyes. Nevertheless, even experienced fly fishermen sometimes lose a fish because the hook is not properly set.

The novice angler often has the image of the fish taking a huge bite that encompasses the fly—but that is not usually the case. Some game fish literally "inhale" the fly, along with a good quantity of water, and once inside the mouth, it is up to the angler to set the hook. Even predators will often take a minnow sideways, and then run for a bit before turning it head-on to swallow. Smaller fish tend to nibble at loose ends of bait or fly, rather than taking the whole in their mouths at once. The fish is not caught as soon as he takes your fly—but you have been given the opportunity to catch him.

Alertness in watching your fly is

essential. Even if the fish has been fooled sufficiently by the *appearance* of your fly to strike, the second it is in his mouth he knows better and will spit it out. You have to strike, so to speak, at the moment of deception.

More fish are lost by striking too slowly than too quickly. You cannot set a hook properly if you have too much slack line out; the force of lifting your rod is dissipated in straightening the line, and your fish will be off. For the same reason, if line slips through your fingers (or off the reel) as you strike, you won't be able to set the hook.

Quick response and a tight line are your best assurances of setting the hook properly.

Detecting the fish's strike is more difficult in subsurface fishing with wet flies and streamers. It is easy to be fooled by a small bump on your fly that might be a piece of grass or a trophy fish. While a game fish will sometimes take the fly and run with it, he may also move *toward* you, in which case you will feel an absolutely slack line after an initial bump.

Learning to interpret the sensations that come to you through your rod is entirely a matter of experience. The novice will have numerous opportunities to feel foolish. In which case about the only recommendation is the old aphorism "Good judgment comes from experience, and experience comes from bad judgment."

PLAYING THE FISH

Once you have set the hook—and the fish knows it—he will generally run. *Let him run.* You should give him as much line as he wants on his initial run, at the same time keeping a rea-sonable tension on the line so he cannot simply shake the hook out of his mouth.

The fish is reacting against your pressure. If the pressure is too strong, he will fight against it. If you don't exert too much resistance, he can even "forget" he is hooked, and will stop running when tired. Then you can begin to retrieve line.

During this initial phase, keep your rod tip high. The flexibility of the rod will keep a steady pressure on without much effort from you. The resistance of the rod will be quite enough to tire the fish. But if he runs suddenly, *drop your rod tip* to point directly at him.

The same tactic is used if the fish jumps out of the water. When he jumps, point your rod tip at him to reduce strain on the tippet. (This is called "bowing" to the fish.) When he is back in the water, bring your tip up again to establish a tight line.

The general rule is: "If the fish wants line, give it to him; if he doesn't, you take it."

As soon as possible, you should eliminate any loops of loose line, and play the fish from the reel, rather than from your hand. If the fish's first run has been powerful enough to run all the fly line off the reel and start on the backing, your first priority is to get fly line back on the reel. It is more difficult to play a fish off the backing (with its small diameter) than from the more easily handled fly line.

If he runs again, don't try to hold him. Give him as much line as he wants when he makes a run. When he stops, you can begin to reel in again.

When he has stopped, pull back

with the rod, then reel in as you drop the tip. *Don't give the fish slack by dropping the tip; reel in quickly.* Repeat this pumping motion, getting as much line back on the reel as you can each time. But be very ready to let go the reel handle *instantly* if he begins another run.

The point through all of this is to maintain a steady tension on the line, without exerting enough pressure either to bend the hook or break your tippet. Unless the fish is very small, "muscling" him in is simply not going to work. You must allow enough time for him to tire himself by working against the resistance of your rod.

A very common error among beginners is to try to land the fish before he is ready to be landed. Be patient! Patient enough to let him tire before you try to land him.

LANDING THE FISH

As the fish tires and you are able to reel in, take in line until there is approximately a rod length (or a foot more) between rod tip and fish. Then, by raising the rod high and back, you can bring him directly to your feet. *This length of line gives you the maximum possible control over the situation.* Longer line gives the fish too much freedom, and shorter makes it likely that you will lift the fish directly

Keep the tip up—but
if fish runs or jumps,
"bow" to him

out of the water, putting too much strain on the tippet.

A small fish can be beached this way, or brought to the edge of the boat. Beaching is one of the surest ways of landing a fish, as every flip of his tail will drive him farther up the beach.

Netting a fish is one of the most common ways of landing, but it is also an enterprise that has put severe strain on many friendships. A lot of fish have been lost at the net, and there is nothing more frustrating than playing a fish well, only to lose him to your

partner's clumsiness with the net. And it happens more often than any of us like to recall. Here are a few points to remember:

1. Don't try to net a fish until he's ready.
2. Don't plunge the net under the fish; *guide* the fish over the net.
3. Net headfirst—and *don't strike the tippet.*

If the angler has the proper amount of line out, he will be able to guide the fish smoothly over the net. But nothing will spook a hooked fish more than someone splashily plunging a net into the water beside him.

If you try to net him tail first, a large fish will often get leverage on the net rim itself as he lashes his tail. At the last moment, the angler can drop his rod tip 6 inches or so, to insure that the net doesn't collide with a taut tippet and throw the fish out.

Never let your partner, no matter how willing, try to net a fish when you still have a lot of line out. This will lead to a great deal of lunging and splashing, and very seldom to a netted fish.

RELEASING THE FISH

A dead fish provides no sport. The purpose of releasing your catch is to return him *undamaged* to the water so he can be caught again.

The key here is the word "undamaged." A fish has been net-battered during landing, mishandled in the boat, gaffed, or otherwise mistreated is not likely to survive, making his release only a hypocritical gesture.

It takes more skill to return a fish safely than to kill him. You will find fishing with barbless hooks a big advantage here. *There are no disadvantages to fishing with barbless*

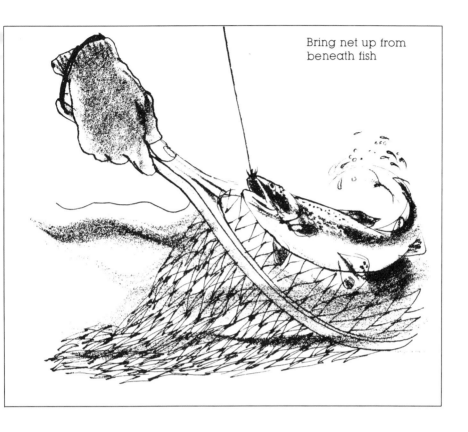

Bring net up from
beneath fish

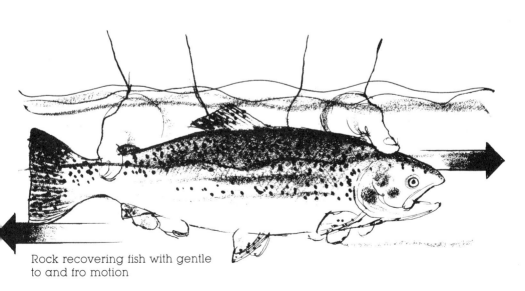

Rock recovering fish with gentle
to and fro motion

hooks. It has been demonstrated again and again that more fish can be properly hooked with a barbless hook than with a barbed one.

You can demonstrate this for yourself by pressing a barbed and a barbless hook into a piece of cardboard. Which hook penetrates more easily?

Hooks can be debarbed by (carefully) smashing the barb flat with pliers. Be careful not to deform the point, and you will have a more effective hook that is easier to dislodge for releasing.

Many fish are killed simply by mishandling. After the excitement of a good fight, it is sometimes difficult to be gentle with a landed fish—*but it is essential.*

You should spend the absolute minimum of time with the fish out of water, and he should be handled as little as possible. If you are going to photograph the catch, *do it quickly.*

A fish cannot usually just be thrown back into the water and survive. He has been exhausted by his fight to escape, and he has used all his resources. In particular, his blood has been deoxygenated by the fight; *you must help him re-establish his life processes.*

When you have carefully removed the hook, cradle the fish with both hands under his belly. Most frequently he will be lying rather still and torpid. Slowly move him backward and forward just under the surface, forcing water through his gills until he begins to show signs of life. This is a highly important step that is often neglected.

When he has recovered enough to swim, he'll let you know, at which point you can release him with your blessings. The more satisfying a fish was to catch, the more satisfying his release.

The days of limitless fish are gone forever. Catch-and-release is the only way our sport can be preserved.

FLY FISHING FOR BASS

The voracious largemouth bass is probably the most popular game fish in America. And when fished on a fly rod, he provides some of the most exciting fishing on the continent. The fly fisherman who doesn't go after bass misses a wonderful treat. And in turn, the bass fisherman who doesn't occasionally try the fly rod on his favorite quarry, passes up a chance for some of the most exciting fishing available.

The popularity of bass is partly due to the fact that no freshwater fish has a wider distribution. From southern Canada to South America, you are never very far from good largemouth bass fishing. Smallmouth bass are also superb fighters, but they like slightly cooler water, and are not so ever-present.

A hungry bass is inclined to eat anything that moves. Their stomachs have yielded small mice, squirrels,

---

ANGLER'S HINT

A coating of Pliobond glue on knots joining leader and fly line and backing and fly line will prevent the knots from hanging up in the guides.

even birds, as well as a more conventional diet of bugs, worms, nymphs, and small baitfish.

The warmer the water, the larger the bass grows. While a 4 or 5 pounder may be large in a northern lake, warm southern waters regularly produce 10 pounders and better. The current world-record largemouth is still the 22 pound, 4 ounce fish taken in Georgia in 1932. However, several 20-plus pound largemouth have been taken in California in recent years, and the next world-record may well come from the West Coast.

Water temperature is a key factor in all fishing, but nowhere is it more important than with bass. The most productive fishing occurs just after the bass have spawned, and this varies according to the temperature.

Largemouth bass spawn when the water reaches the low to mid-60s. In Florida the female often deposits her eggs as early as February, while a Minnesota largemouth may not spawn until mid-June. The fishing season for any given region usually begins shortly after the local spawning period has ended.

Water temperature also has a considerable influence on bass behavior, and, by implication, on your fishing technique. On hot summer days, bass normally feed around dawn and a few hours after. They are also active the last few hours of daylight, when the temperature has cooled a bit and the sunlight is not so bright.

Bass are found in areas of the water with considerable vegetation *and* cover. The majority probably spend their time near the edge of the water, among reeds, grasses, and other aquatic plants. Fallen logs, points, and bridge abutments are also likely spots.

The dry fly, while it can sometimes be deadly, is not the first choice for bass fishing. Bass bugs and poppers are the number-one fish takers. These are larger than the flies tied for trout, and a bass bug dressed on a large hook (1/0 or 2/0) is not unusual.

Poppers are a surface lure, designed to be skipped along in a series of fairly quick retrieves. The original poppers were made of balsa wood for a light float, but most are now plastic.

A great deal of ingenuity has gone into the design of poppers, both in shape and color. It is one of those debates whose answer is always on the local level. Find out first what the local fishermen are using in the way of color, and make your choices from there.

Bass flies are a rather specialized group. Here are a few generally good recommendations:

1. Popping Bug
2. Pusher Bug (hair bug)
3. Prismatic Streamer
4. Leech
5. Dahlberg Diver

BASS FLIES

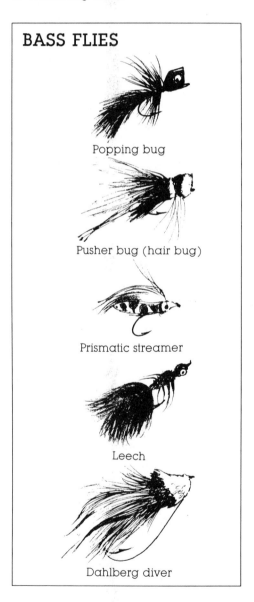

Popping bug

Pusher bug (hair bug)

Prismatic streamer

Leech

Dahlberg diver

Other good fly patterns for bass are the inevitable Muddler Minnow and the Wooly Worm, again in the larger sizes. Streamers and bucktails have proved effective, particularly some of the Marabou streamers.

One rig that is characteristic of bass fishing is the combination of a fly and a tiny spinner just ahead of it. The spinner, which may be as small as your thumbnail, acts as an attractor, getting the bass's attention directed to the fly.

The heavy growth that usually accompanies bass grounds has led to the development of weedless lures, and they can save a good deal of frustration. With a weedless hook, a couple of moderately stiff projections from the head form a sort of skid that allows the hook to pass over vegetation without hooking every piece. They don't interfere with the strike.

Working the fly for bass differs somewhat from trout techniques. Poppers are worked not only for appearance but for sound. The shape of a plastic popper makes it move very jerkily on the retrieve, as well as creating a distinct sound as the flat head intersects the water.

Generally speaking, the fly that is cast for bass should be allowed to remain *unmoving* for a longer time. It is estimated that 60 percent of bass strikes are made on a still fly. Joe Brooks used to allow a full half-minute or minute of dead drift before he would begin to retrieve. Sometimes, he said, it would seem like an hour, but it was the only way.

Between each retrieve, you should allow another long period to elapse before stripping again. Bass tend to look over your fly for some time before making a decision about it. And the warmer the water, *the longer he will take.* The bass in warm water is sometimes a little sluggish to take action—but when he does, it's ferocious!

Many bass fisherman also swear by "teasing" the fish with repeated casts over the area where you think he's holding. When a bass strikes, it often seems to be more out of anger than hunger (though reading the mind of the fish is a very precarious occupation). Teasing can sometimes bring a lazy lunker up for a strike when nothing else works.

It's generally agreed that *the slower you fish a bass bug, the better the results.*

The most common error, even by experienced anglers, is probably fishing too fast. The novice will generally snatch his fly away before the bass has a chance to get a good look at it.

SALTWATER FISHING

Fly fishing on saltwater is still a relatively new sport, at least in popularity. Actually, there was a good deal of light-tackle saltwater fishing a century ago, but it was only after World War II that it became widespread enough to develop a whole set of flies specially designed and tied for the purpose.

Almost every variety of tackle and fly used for freshwater fishing has been adapted to the salt at some time. However, if you spend a significant amount of time on saltwater fishing, you will find yourself in another range of tackle entirely.

Line weights of 8 to 10 are most common, while fishermen going after the really large game fish may use even heavier. A shooting taper is ideal for the long-distance casts.

The saltwater fly rod is also proportionately larger, 9 to 9½ feet, with a slow action. This powerful rod and slow action are required to cast the larger, more wind-resistant flies used on the salt.

The saltwater reel is also different. While your freshwater reel is only used for storing line, a saltwater reel needs an effective drag mechanism for fighting the larger fish. If the fight extends to an hour or so (not uncommon with a large fish), a well-set drag can save you an incredible amount of energy.

The saltwater reel needs to carry a large amount of backing. For general fishing, your reel should be able to carry 250 yards of 18-pound test nylon in addition to your fly line. Compared to a freshwater fish, the run of an ocean dweller is long, hard, and often unobstructed. A large tarpon, for example, can strip off a hundred yards of backing almost before you know he's hooked.

When fishing for some species, like barracuda, a shock tippet of light wire can be the only way to catch the fish. The abrasion of sharp teeth on a monofilament tippet will almost always lose the fish. The International Game Fish Association classifies world records under tippet strengths. They recognize fish caught on 6-pound, 10-pound, 12-pound, and 15-pound tippets as separate records.

The number of different species fished for in saltwater has grown rapidly in recent years. The pioneers of the sport fished for snook, tarpon, ladyfish, and red drum. Bonefish, barracuda, permit, and others were added later, as the sport gained popularity. On both coasts striped bass have become major angling targets.

Popping bugs in large sizes (say, a 3/0 hook) are often used on the salt, as well as baitfish-imitating streamers such as the famous series of Blondes originated by Joe Brooks.

The popping bug is fished in much the same manner as you would use for largemouth bass. Pop it once, let it sit for a good period, then pop again, sit again, and bring it back in a series of pops. This general strategy seems to work as well with the popping bug on saltwater as it does in fresh.

The large streamers and bucktails are retrieved with 1- or 2-foot jerks. They should be allowed to sink well below the surface, and kept in more constant motion than a popping bug. A saltwater streamer should be about 4 inches in length, and they are tied on both 3/0 and 5/0 hooks.

Cam's Half-Dozen

1. Skipping bug
2. Brooks's blonde series
3. Lefty's deceiver
4. Tarpon fly
5. Bonefish fly
6. Pink shrimp

Again, every area has its own specialties, both in technique and the kind of fly that produces the most consistent results. There is a very wide difference between fishing bonefish in

CAM'S HALF-DOZEN SALTWATER FLIES

Skipping bug

Joe Brooks's Blonde series

Lefty's Deceiver

Tarpon fly

Bonefish fly

Pink shrimp

the shallow waters of the Florida Keys, and striped bass in Northern California.

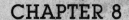

CHAPTER 8

AMERICAN FISH

No country in the world offers a wider range of fishing than the United States. The sheer variety of freshwater fishing is unequalled, from tiny farm ponds to great reservoirs, from the slow Eastern rivers to the high mountain streams of the West. And in addition there are many thousands of miles of saltwater coastline; two great oceans and the Gulf of Mexico provide endless opportunities for the saltwater fly rodder.

THE TROUT FAMILY

For the fly fisherman, the trout family is unquestionably the most sought quarry. While almost every fish has been taken on a fly at some time, so popular is the trout that in many people's minds, fly fishing and trout fishing are one and the same.

The range of trout in the United States is not restricted to the popular image of high mountain streams. Unless polluted, most cold waters support some variety of trout. While many varieties exist, the majority of trout fishing is the pursuit of the following four main species.

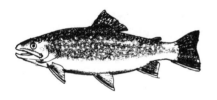

BROOK TROUT

BROOK TROUT *(Salvelinus fontinalis)*
Brook trout (sometimes called speckled trout) are generally considered the easiest to catch. Brookies (actually a species of char) are an American species, native in the Northeast from Georgia to the Arctic Circle. Although the brook trout has been planted in many other regions than its native one, it does not seem to be as adaptable as its cousins, the brown and rainbow.

The best fishing for the brook trout is still in its native regions, particularly from New England north into Canada. Despite its dwindling habitat, it is still considered one of the principal game fish in New England, and fisheries management programs tend to favor the brookie over other trout.

BROWN TROUT

BROWN TROUT *(Salmo trutta)*
The brown is the native trout of Europe, where it is found all the way from the Mediterranean north into Arctic Norway. It was imported into the U.S. in the 1880s, and owing to its vigorous ability to adapt, has become firmly established throughout the country.

The brown is notoriously difficult to catch. In experiments where browns were stocked equally with rainbows, it was found that anglers could take only one brown for every four or five rainbows from the same water. Browns have the greatest tolerance for warm water of any trout, sometimes being found in water up to 75 degrees.

While the world record brown trout is over 30 pounds, the majority caught in the U.S. weigh a pound or under.

RAINBOW TROUT

RAINBOW TROUT *(Salmo gairdneri)*
Another native American, the rainbow is renowned as a fighter. They usually leap when hooked, and put up a magnificent battle.

The rainbow exists in two forms, the nonmigratory and the anadromous (or sea-going), known to all Western anglers as the "steelhead." The range of these superb sportfish is all the way from California to the Aleutian Islands. Migratory steelhead are entering Pacific Coast rivers at all times of the year.

While the steelhead is native to the Pacific Coast, it has been successfully introduced into the Great Lakes region, and has become a major game fish there.

Nonmigratory rainbows exhibit considerable variation in appearance, and the characteristic red band along the side (for which the fish is named), only appears in the mature fish. The migratory steelhead in the ocean have few or no spots and are silver-sided. As they proceed up the rivers for spawning they become darker and spotted, and the red band appears.

CUTTHROAT TROUT

THE CUTTHROAT *(Salmo clarki)*
The cutthroat is also an American native, with a range from northern California to Alaska, and inland throughout the Western United States and Canada. This species, like the rainbow, has both a nonmigratory and an anadromous variety.

The cutthroat is named for the bright orange or red slashes under the jawbone, which are quite faint in the immature fish but become very vivid in the mature adult.

The cutthroat's water preference is very similar to that of the rainbow,

and in fact, the two species frequently hybridize in the streams and high lakes of Wyoming and Montana. The hybrids have the general appearance of the rainbow (including the reddish band), but are identifiable by the unmistakable red slashes of the cutthroat.

THE BASS FAMILY

The different varieties of bass are the most important game fish on the continent. More people fish for bass than any other fish, and by a considerable margin.

In part this is due to the bass family's extraordinary adaptability. It has proven its ability to survive in almost any freshwater environment, pond, lake, or stream, and as a result is one of the most widely distributed species in the U.S.

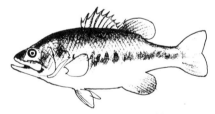

LARGEMOUTH BASS

LARGEMOUTH BASS *(Micropterus salmoides)*
Except for some areas in the northern mountain states, the largemouth bass is found everywhere in the country, sometimes under a variety of local names, including black bass and bucketmouth.

Part of the secret of the largemouth's enormously wide distribution is the fact that he is far from a fussy eater. The diet of the largemouth is probably more varied than that of any other fish. Insects, larva, small fish, crayfish, frogs, snakes, and even mice fall prey to his voracious appetite.

Because of this, the largemouth is fished in almost every imaginable way. Fly rodding (with bass bugs), jigging, surface lures, spinnerbaits, and the ever-present plastic worm are all favorite methods in some part of the country.

The largemouth is rarely found in water more than 20 feet deep, and almost never leaves areas with rooted vegetation. Bass from northern, cooler waters seldom attain the size of southern bass.

SMALLMOUTH BASS *(Micropterus dolomieui)*

The smallmouth bass is not as widely distributed as his cousin, the largemouth. The smallmouth's original distribution was in the north-central portions of the country. Until about 1870, in fact, its range was largely restricted to the Lake Ontario and Ohio River drainages.

SMALLMOUTH BASS

The coming of the railroads changed all that, however, as smallmouth were planted in streams all over the country. On occasion the method was as simple as carrying a bucket of fish in the water tender of the locomotive!

As a result, there were a number of widely scattered plantings, some of which survived and some of which did not.

The main distinguishing charac-

teristic of the smallmouth bass is that the upper jaw does not project behind the eye of the fish, as it does in the largemouth. It has a coppery-olive sheen to the sides, which sometimes gives it the local name of bronzeback.

Its fighting ability is so respected that, in the South, the smallmouth is sometimes called "green trout."

Smallmouth prefer deeper, more rocky environments than do the largemouth, and somewhat cooler waters. In lakes, smallmouth often form fairly large schools, while river and stream dwellers are, for the most part, loners.

Smallmouth will normally be found in the same locations year-round. You may have to change your fishing tactics with the season, but once you've found a good hole, the fish will be there.

THE PANFISH

To some sportsmen it will seem odd to include the lowly panfish in the category of game fish. But more pure sport has probably been had with these innocuous little flat fish than all other species combined.

The term "panfish" covers a broad spectrum of small fish, most of which belong to the sunfish family. Bream, crappies, bluegill, and yellow perch are probably the most common names across the country. Local names abound, with crappies alone having more than fifty titles like "strawberry bass" and "papermouth."

Make no mistake about the panfish. When worked with tackle of appropriate size he can be as interesting a fish to fight as any of his more romantic cousins. With some of the new ultralight tackle, you'd believe you had a largemouth bass on the other end. And above all, of course, the little panfish are superb eating.

BLUEGILLS AND CRAPPIES

The bluegill, known in the South as "bream," is the most widely distributed fish in the country. As with bass, the largest are found in warm southern waters. Bluegills are easily identified by the powder blue tint on the bottom of the gill cover.

The bluegill diet of insects, larvae, and small crustaceans makes them a reasonable target for the fly fisherman with a wet fly (though the most popular lure is a small popping bug). While they usually hold to shallow water around vegetation, in midsummer they may be found as deep as 20 feet.

Bluegills and crappies both have a tendency to severely overpopulate, leading to numerous but very small fish. As a result, the larger fish will always be taken in areas that are not too densely populated.

PERCH

Perch are a more northern fish, closely related to walleyes and saugers. Where bluegills and crappies spawn in water temperatures of 64 to 68 degrees, the yellow perch begins spawning at about 45 degrees. In the North, perch are a favorite of ice fishermen.

Perch, like most panfish, can withstand very heavy fishing pressure. A lake overpopulated with perch will never produce individuals of sufficient size to interest the angler. Eight or 9 inches is a reasonable catch. A

giant of over 4 pounds was taken in New Jersey—in 1865—and remains the world record.

Panfish need to be fished more slowly than the athletic fish like trout and bass. They will hover near bait or lure for a long time, looking it over, and are easily spooked by splashes and sounds. However, the same fish that darted away when your lure landed on the water, may well come back to take it if you leave it still and unthreatening on the surface.

SALTWATER FISH

With our two long seacoasts and the Gulf of Mexico, there is plenty of angling available for the saltwater fly rodder. This is a field that is just coming into its own. We don't really know yet how many ocean-dwellers will take a fly. Since in many cases insects are not a part of their normal diet, we frequently don't even know *why* they will take a fly.

Saltwater fly fishing is an exciting field for the innovator, the experimenter. Some of the records still on the books occurred simply because the angler was the first person ever to throw a fly at that particular fish. (One of the authors of this book held the world record for bluefish for a short time, for just that reason.)

BONEFISH

The bonefish is a 30-mile-per-hour fish, and therein lies his great attraction. The initial run of a hooked bonefish is breathtaking in its power and speed.

Bonefish feed on shallow flats, coming in at flood tide to forage the

BONEFISH

bottom, and retreating to deeper water as the tide goes out. They are usually fished either by wading, or from a flat skiff poled by a guide. The skiff allows you to cover much more area in a day, and present your fly to many more fish.

As bonefish forage head-down in the shallows, their tails frequently break the surface of the water in the phenomenon called "tailing." While they are a school fish, groups as small as four or five, or even isolated individuals, can be spotted.

When spooked, however, the whole school will react as a unit. It has been said that bonefishing is the only game in town where you can scare a hundred fish with one bad cast. Careful stalking is the name of the game.

TARPON

Fly rodding for the giant tarpon is considered by many experienced fishermen to be the ultimate angling thrill. If you can imagine a 100-pound explosion on the end of a sensitive rod, you can easily understand why.

Like bonefish, tarpon are found in most subtropical and tropical waters. The water fished is usually not over 8 feet deep. Bucktails and streamers, particularly those that are dressed to "breathe" on the retrieve, are favorite flies with tarpon fishermen.

The tarpon's explosive leap is his signature. They've been known to go 8 feet straight up and 20 feet horizontally. While tarpon are known to reach 300 pounds, most fish caught are under 100 pounds. Some aficionados of the sport, however, say that the best day's fishing is when you tie into a school of 10 to 20 pounders, which can give you more action than you're prepared for. Needless to say, your gear must be heavy and suited to the task.

SPORT FISHING IN THE UNITED STATES

The maps on the following pages will give you a quick guide to the distribution of these species.

NORTHEAST

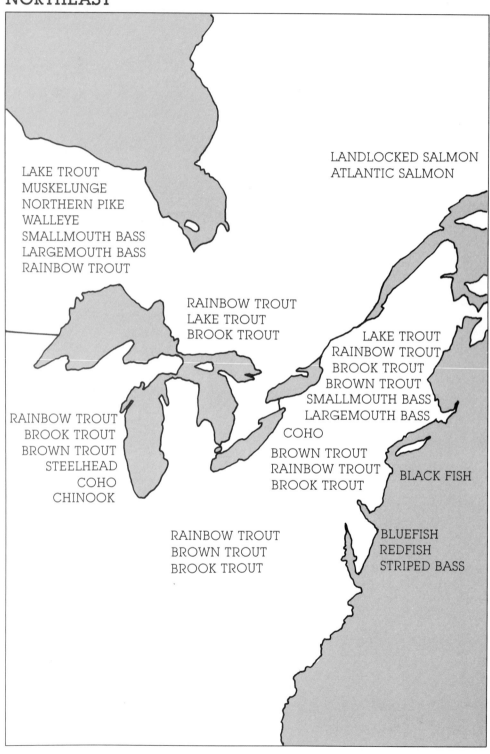

LAKE TROUT
MUSKELUNGE
NORTHERN PIKE
WALLEYE
SMALLMOUTH BASS
LARGEMOUTH BASS
RAINBOW TROUT

LANDLOCKED SALMON
ATLANTIC SALMON

RAINBOW TROUT
LAKE TROUT
BROOK TROUT

LAKE TROUT
RAINBOW TROUT
BROOK TROUT
BROWN TROUT
SMALLMOUTH BASS
LARGEMOUTH BASS

COHO

RAINBOW TROUT
BROOK TROUT
BROWN TROUT
STEELHEAD
COHO
CHINOOK

BROWN TROUT
RAINBOW TROUT
BROOK TROUT

BLACK FISH

RAINBOW TROUT
BROWN TROUT
BROOK TROUT

BLUEFISH
REDFISH
STRIPED BASS

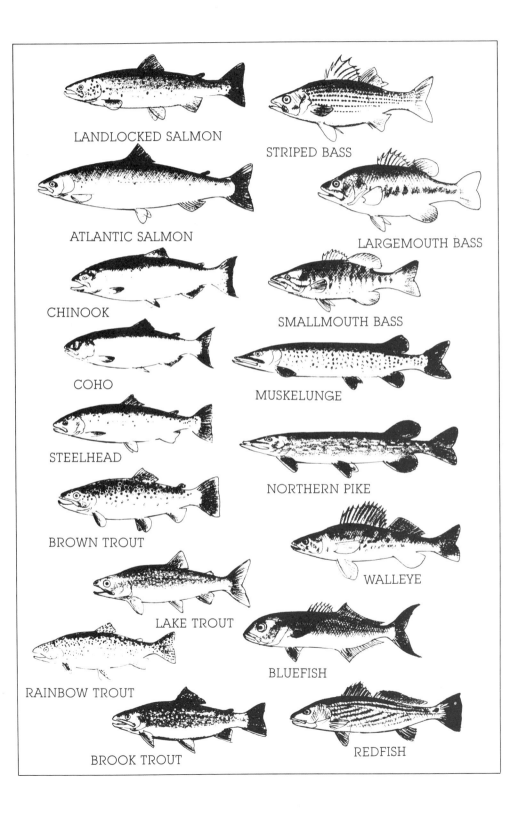

LANDLOCKED SALMON

STRIPED BASS

ATLANTIC SALMON

LARGEMOUTH BASS

CHINOOK

SMALLMOUTH BASS

COHO

MUSKELUNGE

STEELHEAD

NORTHERN PIKE

BROWN TROUT

WALLEYE

LAKE TROUT

BLUEFISH

RAINBOW TROUT

BROOK TROUT

REDFISH

SOUTHEAST

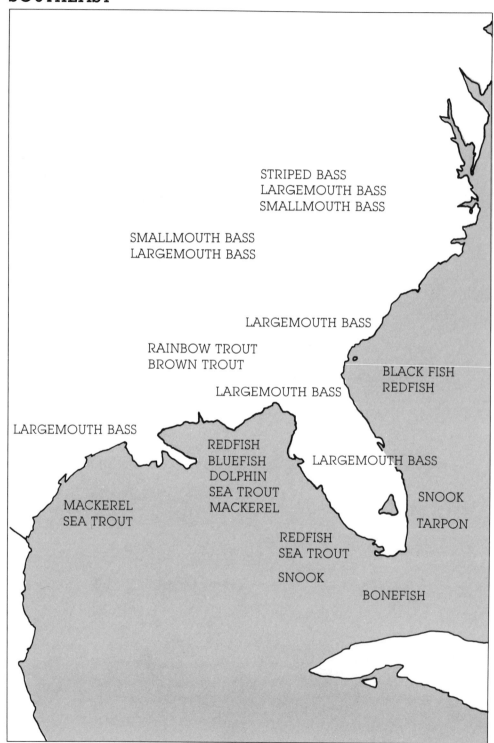

STRIPED BASS
LARGEMOUTH BASS
SMALLMOUTH BASS

SMALLMOUTH BASS
LARGEMOUTH BASS

LARGEMOUTH BASS

RAINBOW TROUT
BROWN TROUT

BLACK FISH
REDFISH

LARGEMOUTH BASS

LARGEMOUTH BASS

REDFISH
BLUEFISH
DOLPHIN
SEA TROUT
MACKEREL

LARGEMOUTH BASS

SNOOK

MACKEREL
SEA TROUT

TARPON

REDFISH
SEA TROUT

SNOOK

BONEFISH

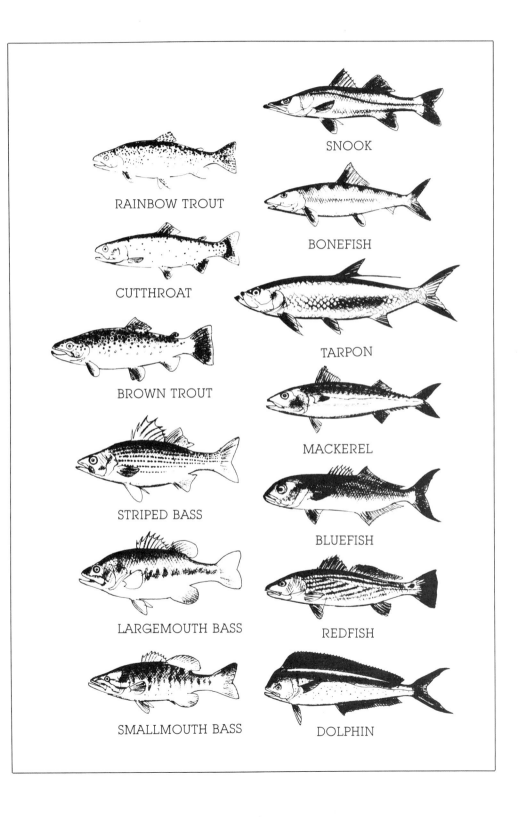

SNOOK

RAINBOW TROUT

BONEFISH

CUTTHROAT

TARPON

BROWN TROUT

MACKEREL

STRIPED BASS

BLUEFISH

LARGEMOUTH BASS

REDFISH

SMALLMOUTH BASS

DOLPHIN

SOUTHWEST

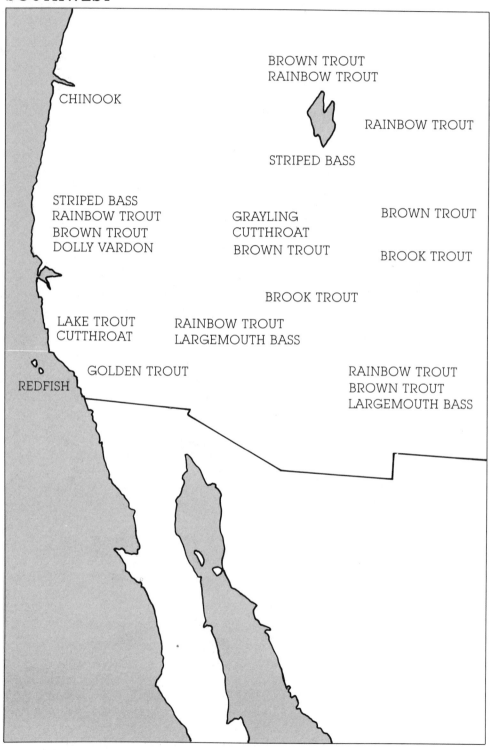

BROWN TROUT
RAINBOW TROUT

CHINOOK

RAINBOW TROUT

STRIPED BASS

STRIPED BASS
RAINBOW TROUT
BROWN TROUT
DOLLY VARDON

GRAYLING
CUTTHROAT
BROWN TROUT

BROWN TROUT

BROOK TROUT

BROOK TROUT

LAKE TROUT
CUTTHROAT

RAINBOW TROUT
LARGEMOUTH BASS

GOLDEN TROUT

RAINBOW TROUT
BROWN TROUT
LARGEMOUTH BASS

REDFISH

CHINOOK

GOLDEN TROUT

RAINBOW TROUT

BROOK TROUT

CUTTHROAT

GRAYLING

DOLLY VARDON

STRIPED BASS

BROWN TROUT

LARGEMOUTH BASS

LAKE TROUT

SMALLMOUTH BASS

NORTHWEST

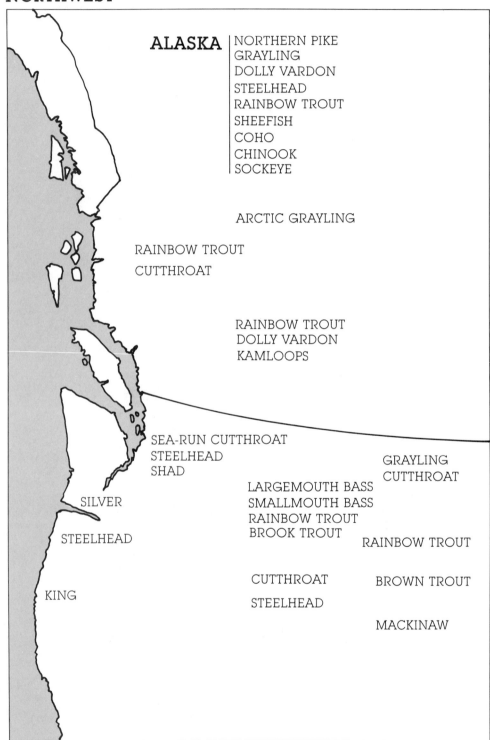

ALASKA | NORTHERN PIKE
GRAYLING
DOLLY VARDON
STEELHEAD
RAINBOW TROUT
SHEEFISH
COHO
CHINOOK
SOCKEYE

ARCTIC GRAYLING

RAINBOW TROUT

CUTTHROAT

RAINBOW TROUT
DOLLY VARDON
KAMLOOPS

SEA-RUN CUTTHROAT
STEELHEAD
SHAD

GRAYLING
CUTTHROAT

LARGEMOUTH BASS
SMALLMOUTH BASS
RAINBOW TROUT
BROOK TROUT

SILVER

RAINBOW TROUT

STEELHEAD

CUTTHROAT

BROWN TROUT

KING

STEELHEAD

MACKINAW

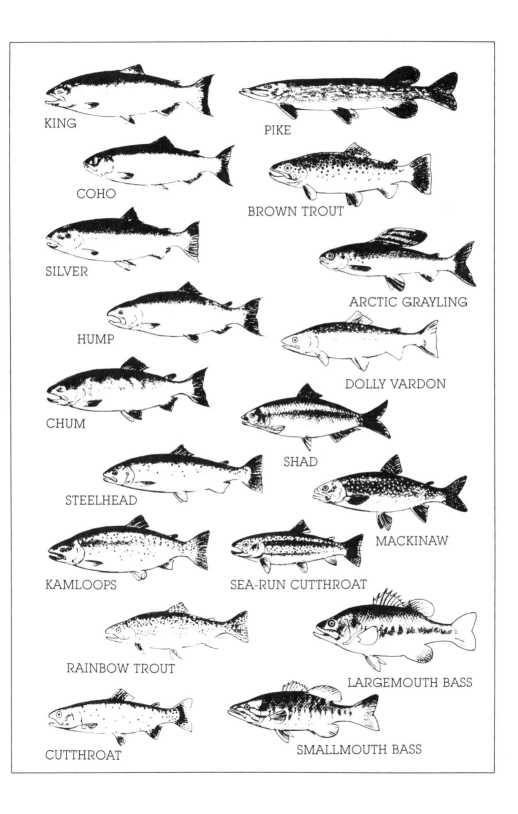

KING

PIKE

COHO

BROWN TROUT

SILVER

ARCTIC GRAYLING

HUMP

DOLLY VARDON

CHUM

SHAD

STEELHEAD

MACKINAW

KAMLOOPS

SEA-RUN CUTTHROAT

RAINBOW TROUT

LARGEMOUTH BASS

CUTTHROAT

SMALLMOUTH BASS

Flyfishing

PART IV
WHERE TO GO

CHAPTER 9

BACK COUNTRY PACK-IN

The combination of backpacking and fly fishing is a marriage made in heaven. Many of the most positive elements of fishing—contact with unspoiled nature, solitude, alertness to the world around you—are intensified immeasurably on a backpacking trip.

Most of us in modern America are totally dependent on the automobile; dependent to such a degree that we tolerate the fumes, the noise, the inconvenience without even a second thought. And even when we are seeking the "natural," the habit runs deep. The freedom to move great distances rapidly has replaced virtually every other aspect of traveling.

Imagine this: some years ago the Yellowstone Park Company surveyed travelers in our first and most famous national park. They discovered that an astounding 70 percent of visitors passed through without getting out of their cars!

Another 29 percent indicated that they spent some time out of their cars observing the famous natural features of the park, but *only when they were visible from the road.*

Worse than you thought? Or maybe *better* than you thought. Because it means that in this two-million-acre park, notoriously overcrowded in the season, only 1 percent of the visitors ever get more than a few yards off the road.

The same is true in greater or lesser degree for every park, national forest, or wilderness area in the country. The overcrowding, and the consequent fishing pressure, is limited to the areas that can be reached directly by automobile.

What a priceless gift this is to the angler who is willing to hike a little! And even more to the backpacker. It is easy to convert our automobile habit into rich opportunity for the highest-quality fishing.

It is safe to say there are tens of thousands of choice fishing spots in this country that are unfished because they lie a mile off the road. In many cases, even a few hundred yards are enough to completely lose the trappings and the annoyances of "civilized" life.

The point is that backpacking need not always be considered in terms of a major expedition, a test of endurance or hardiness. Because the majority of people stick so closely to the main roads, there is a vast *range* of experience possible. It simply depends on how much energy you want to put into it.

Backpacking for the sake of fishing is not the same thing as backpacking for the sake of hiking. The angler doesn't care how many miles he logs in a day, as long as he can find good fishing. The point is not in the quantity of land covered, but in the quality of the experience.

When you realize that a couple of hours on the trail may transport you back a hundred years in time, to an era of peaceful, natural beauty, the investment seems small.

FISHING GEAR FOR BACKPACKING

In recent years, virtually every major manufacturer of fishing tackle has offered equipment that is specially designed for the backpacker. The quality ranges from poor to excellent, but by choosing gear from a reputable manufacturer you will have no difficulty outfitting yourself with a fine kit.

The only substantial difference is in the design of the rod. A pack rod is usually in four sections (five in the case of a long fly rod), and will pack into a tube approximately 2 feet long.

At one time, these multiple-section rods were distinctly inferior in action to their one- or two-piece counterparts. The early pack rods used metal ferrules for connecting the sections, which broke up the smooth delivery of power.

The development of ferrules of

the same material as the rod, either Fiberglas or graphite, has largely corrected those early defects. A four-section rod from a reputable manufacturer should give you entirely satisfactory service.

Pack rods are available either as single-purpose fly or spinning rods, with appropriate reels. However, the workhorse of pack rods is a combination rod, which can be used either for spin casting with small lures, or fly casting.

In spite of myths to the contrary, most expert fly fishermen are not "purists," in the sense that they refuse to fish with anything but a fly. They are fishermen who prefer the fly when they can use it intelligently but will certainly fish with the kind of equipment that is most appropriate to the situation.

Particularly in backpacking, it would seem a rather foolish posture to insist on one kind of equipment for its own sake. The combination rod means you will have to carry two reels, but will at least double your chances for taking fish.

For the average fishing, a combination rod of about 7½ feet is about right. Most of your fly casting will be on comparatively small streams or lakes, and you will probably not find the shorter length a serious handicap. Most pack rods are balanced with 4 to 6 weight fly line.

The case in which your rod is packed is very important. The best is an aluminum tube that will withstand years of knocking about without allowing damage to the rod. Some manufacturers provide sturdy tubes as part of their pack rod kit, while others have fiber or vinyl cases.

If your rod does not come with an aluminum tube, *get one.* Over a period of time the freedom from worry it will provide is well worth an extra ounce or two.

The reels you currently use will probably do perfectly well for your backpacking kit—with one exception. If you have a particularly precious reel, we would advise buying an inexpensive one for your backpacking expeditions. Backpacking gear is subject to more than ordinary hazards over a period of time, and there is no use worrying about a prized possession in the back country.

If you have opted for a combination spin/fly kit, you should carry an extra spool of line for your spinning reel. Tangles happen to the best, line never gets any longer, and that extra spool is cheap insurance.

You should carry a reasonable selection of leaders, and probably a separate spool or two of tippet material. These are the parts of your kit most subject to natural attrition, and you have to get used to the fact that you will not be carrying a well-equipped tackle box. For the period of your trip, your vest will serve as tackle box.

Fortunately for our legs, most of our equipment is light. However, it is still necessary to do some intelligent weeding out of gear to make an efficient backpacking kit.

You should not have more than two fly boxes. Plan with as much knowledge as you can gather, and then take only the most likely, best-producing flies for your area. Whatever works most consistently under your normal fishing conditions is also going to be right for the back country.

Backpack fishing places a premium on good organization and efficiency. Most of us accumulate a much wider variety of flies than we actually need ("for special conditions"), as well as gadgets and tools. There are many items that would be delightful to have—if they grew on bushes at streamside—but aren't really worth carrying and keeping track of. Keep it simple.

BACKPACKING GEAR

The technology of fabrics and materials has revolutionized backpacking in the past couple of decades. Everything from shoes to tents is lighter, more comfortable, and easier to handle.

"Roughing it" is not the point of back country packing. If you want to be miserable, you can certainly find many ways to do that in the city. The idea is to be as comfortable as possible with the minimum of fuss. That balance is one of the peculiar satisfactions of back country fishing.

The two most important elements in your comfort are your sleeping bag and your shoes. Many deficiencies can be accommodated in the course of a trip, but if anything is wrong with either your sleeping bag or your shoes, you will suffer for it more or less continuously.

SLEEPING BAGS
There are two schools of thought on sleeping bags, one favoring the classic goose-down bag, and the other leaning toward the newer, synthetic materials like Fiberfill II or Dacron II.

There is no other material, manmade or natural, that has the insulating properties of goose down. Period. Duck down, which is often available in lower-priced bags, is a poor substitute.

The insulation of a sleeping bag depends on loft, not weight. While most manufacturers tell you how many pounds of down are in their bags, 3 pounds of duck down will never hold its loft like 3 pounds of goose down.

Buy a sleeping bag from a firm that specializes in outdoor outfitting. When such a specialist firm tells you that the bag is good to −10 degrees, you may trust it.

However, goose down has one deficiency that makes a reasonable case possible for the synthetic materials. When down becomes wet, it balls up and loses its capacity to hold air, which is what insulation is all about.

In wet situations, where there is a good chance of your bag becoming saturated, the synthetics perform handsomely. A bag filled with Fiberfill II or Dacron II will retain its insulating properties long after a goose-down bag has become soggy and cold.

The synthetic material will be heavier for the same amount of insulation, and it will not pack as small as a down bag. It will, however, be considerably cheaper than down.

There are other synthetic materials used for cheap sleeping bags, but they are not really worth considering. Neither are the inferior kinds of down. The quality of your sleeping bag is all-important to your comfort, and it is *not* the proper place to cut corners.

FOOTWEAR
Sharing top priority with the sleeping bag in your backpacking comfort is

your footwear. Here again, recent technology has made some significant changes. The new generation of hiking boots is much lighter than the old all-leather variety, break in more easily, and are better insulated. They are superior in almost every way.

Walking with a 40-pound pack imposes different strains on the foot than walking without any additional weight. You need a solid arch support and many people require good ankle support as well. To some degree, it is a question of individual requirements. Good boots can be bought either in a low-top style, or above the ankle.

It only makes sense to try your boots for comfort *while wearing a pack*. Many outdoor outfitters keep a loaded pack handy for just that purpose. Some individuals' feet flatten more under load than others'. A pair of boots that is to be worn under load is not fairly tested without that load.

Most hikers wear two pair of socks, light cotton next to the skin and a heavier woolen pair outside. You should try out boots wearing the same socks you will use on the trail.

Never buy a pair of boots immediately before a trip. It is an almost certain way to spend much of your time nursing blisters. While the newer, softer boots do break in more rapidly than they used to, it still requires time for any boot to adapt to *your* foot.

Before you go out on the trail, wear your boots around the house, down to the store, mowing the lawn. Wear them at every opportunity, to insure that they've had a chance to conform to your feet.

A typical hiking boot with a stiff, Vibram sole designed to bite into the earth, is not the most comfortable

footwear around the camp. In addition, their very efficiency tends to tear up soil at an amazing rate. It has been estimated that four hikers traveling 5 miles will turn over almost a *ton* of soil.

If you can work it into your pack, a pair of tennis shoes or running shoes will be a welcome addition around camp.

TENTS AND PACKS

Generally speaking, camping gear intended for mountaineering is the best bet for the backpacking fly fisherman. When bought by reputable brand name, such equipment will be the lightest and sturdiest available.

The waterproof-but-breathable fabrics like Gore-Tex have led to a new generation of single-piece tents, which are erected without the customary rain fly. Mountain tents of this material come in two-, three-, and sometimes four-man sizes. They are usually constructed as free-standing domes with outside supports (Fiberglas rods), which provide the maximum interior space.

The dome-shaped tent (Gore-Tex or otherwise) is particularly resistant to wind loads, and can often be set up on rocky terrain where getting a stake in the ground is impossible.

Single-piece tents are expensive for the space enclosed, but they do a great deal toward reducing interior condensation, and they *are* waterproof. And, of course, you don't have to deal with a rain fly in addition to the tent itself.

However, before investing in this new tent material, it is worth considering that the traditional rain fly serves other functions in your comfort than shedding rain. A taut rain fly creates a dead air space between your tent wall and the outside air; an insulating barrier several inches deep. This can make the traditional style much easier to heat. Unless you are in really severe conditions, a single candle will warm a two- or three-man mountain tent very comfortably.

In backpacking, the way you can distribute the load is an important factor. If, for example, your angling party is four people, you would be better advised to have two two-man tents than one four-man version.

The best way to evaluate tents is by getting a number of reputable outdoor outfitters' catalogs, and studying the specifications carefully. A few hours of "print study" will allow you to narrow the selection down to fit your particular requirements, and you will approach the job of selecting your back country home with much more confidence.

There is no way of explaining the "feel" of a tent. The shape, color, entrance, all have *something* to do with it, but not everything. But if you feel confined, you are not going to use it as often. It is a very personal thing, and worth spending considerable care in deciding. If you go to a showroom and spend ten minutes sitting inside an erected tent, you may get a funny look or two, but it could make a big difference in your comfort over five or ten years.

While taste varies, a cool-colored tent, blue or green, is usually best. When you look out the flap in the morning, the outside world seems very inviting and urges you to get up and be about your business. Whereas the contrast with a warm-colored tent usually makes the outside seem

somewhat gloomy and forbidding. This is purely a psychological phenomenon, but it does make a difference in your camping experience.

The pack you choose is not as important as the way you pack it. Again, there is such a variety of excellent packs available that the choice becomes a matter of individual taste. The normal recommendations of light frame, easily available outside pockets, and so forth, have pretty well been taken care of by the manufacturers. Pack design has become very sophisticated. The main differences are in style and quality of workmanship, which means durability.

Remember, however, that whatever *size* pack you buy, you are going to fill it to overflowing. If you have a pack with a 70-pound capacity, you are probably going to be packing 70 pounds. It's an unfortunate psychological weakness, but it seems to be just about universal. If there's space left, you'll cram something in it.

For this reason, it's sometimes a good idea *not* to get the largest pack you think you'll ever need, but something a little smaller. Thirty-five pounds is plenty for the average person to carry on a day's hike. Don't be intimidated by stories of packers rushing up mountains with 70-pound loads. You are not going to do that.

The key to packing properly has a lot to do with the way you approach it mentally. Many inexperienced packers start out (in their mind) with a house full of things, and figure how to cut down to what they need. *This is the wrong approach to the problem.*

An old-timer in the Oregon Coast Range once said "the way to pack is to imagine yourself naked in the wilderness. Then, *item by item*, add what you need, and only what you need. Just because a piece of gear is useful doesn't mean you need it."

Anything this woodsman had not used in three trips was eliminated from his pack. He eventually carried less than 20 pounds, and was better equipped—meaning more comfortable—than any of his compatriots. On a short trip of two or three days he could get down to 12 pounds rather easily.

Comfort in backpacking is a matter of strategy, not equipment. The majority of recreational backpackers carry more than they need, and their comfort is reduced proportionately.

BACKPACKER'S HINT

Pay a lot of attention to your own comfort. It's one of the great delights of backpacking to be perfectly comfortable with a minimum of gear. Shoes and sleeping bag are the main priorities.

The actual packing of your gear should proceed by a system of priorities. The rule is "first out, last in." Whatever you will need *first*, should be packed *last*.

For the angler this probably means that your fishing vest should be on the very top of the pack. Many good trails follow the water, and when the purpose of your trip is fishing, you will want to fish as you go. If any essential part of your fishing equipment is buried deep in your pack, it will be too much trouble.

All your tackle should be in your vest. Then it is easy and convenient to try a couple of casts at any likely looking spot along the way.

This rather casual mode of travel is quite at odds with the "got to be at Bear Lake by sundown" school. You are not measuring your trip in miles traversed, but in fishing experience. Sometimes the whole point of the trip is that you don't have to be *anyplace* by any particular time.

The nature of backpacking is that you are "home" wherever you are. It is easy to spoil this freedom by setting a schedule that either strains your endurance or causes you to pass up the kind of experience you really came for: of looking, and listening, and fishing, and enjoying either the solitude or the companionship of your friends.

The success of any backpacking trip revolves around being with like-minded people. The angler who wants to explore the water as he goes, will find himself frustrated if his companions are vigorous time-and-distance hikers. And vice-versa.

For the maximum pleasure in a backpacking trip, it is worth giving considerable thought to your choice of companions. Try to be sure that you are all on the trip for the same kind of experience. It is vastly more important than what kind of equipment you have or don't have.

FIRES AND COOKING
One of the greatest pleasures of the backpacking trip are the meals. This is even more true for the fly fisherman, when he can cook his fish within minutes after it has been caught. It is no secret that the eating quality of a fresh-caught fish is quite different from

one that has been away from the water for any amount of time.

The days of the open campfire, made from gathered wood, are dwindling. While there are still some areas where this is possible, more and more often we run into "no fire" or "fire permit" restrictions. Sometimes these restrictions are for the purpose of avoiding uncontrolled fire in the back country, and sometimes they are to protect the country from the considerable damage that can be done by wood-seeking campers.

In either case, *these restrictions make good sense* and they should be carefully followed by any responsible outdoorsman.

Never count on the possibility of an open campfire. Your camping stove is an essential part of your kit.

Backpacking stoves are now available in several forms, all of which are light, convenient, efficient, and designed for your exact purpose.

The two most common fuels are white gas under pressure, and propane/butane stoves. Either works very well. Your fuel should be carried in sealed containers—nothing is more unpleasant than finding your clothing soaked with white gas at the end of the day.

About the only disadvantage of these cannister-type stoves is that your empty cannister *must be packed out with you!* This is, of course, true of *anything* you bring into the woods. You either eat it or take it back out with you. Leave nothing behind.

The bare minimum of cooking gear is less than you probably think. Nesting pots and pans, again made specifically for backpacking, are very good. However, you can certainly get by with a rather small assortment of ordinary kitchen gear.

A two-quart kettle, a one-quart saucepan, and a 10-inch skillet will handle almost any meal reasonably well. In addition, each member should have his own plate and cup for which he is personally responsible, regardless of how other camp duties are divided.

The selection of lightweight dehydrated foods is now vast beyond anything we could imagine twenty years ago. Freeze-drying, dehydration, and precooking have been applied to almost everything you can eat.

It is an excellent idea to plan the menu for every meal you intend to eat during the trip, and then add some small percentage for emergency delays in your return. This is a commonly recommended practice that is not commonly followed. Nevertheless, it works very well.

CLOTHING

The subject of outdoor clothing for the fisherman has been dealt with in Chapter Four. But a couple of general principles might be added.

In the matter of warmth, you should always follow the "layer" idea.

It is more efficient to put on an extra layer of comparatively light material, than to change entirely to a heavy garment. Not only do you carry less, but you are warmer and much more flexible in the face of changing weather conditions.

In backpacking, you always have two separate conditions to deal with. When you are exerting yourself on the trail, you will be kept warm largely by the heat of your own exertion. But the moment you are in camp, or fishing, you will need to add clothing for warmth.

A good down jacket is probably the most versatile single piece of wearing apparel you can have. It has been home away from home for backpackers since Eddie Bauer first developed it. Nothing else creates such a consistent "climate," regardless of outside conditions. The down jacket has probably made more difference in the comfort of outdoorsmen than any other single factor.

Every outdoor outfitter has a range of down clothing. The initial investment is high, but with proper care you may use it for ten years. Insulated jackets of Fiberfill II and the other synthetics are also generally available. (See the earlier section on sleeping bags for comparative advantages and disadvantages.)

Two schools of thought on down jackets should be mentioned here. One school, represented by the French Terray, believes in the lightest possible taffeta shell surrounding the down. This kind of shell is resistant to *nothing*. Not rain, or abrasion, or any kind of mishandling. It is assumed that an additional waterproof poncho will be worn if it is really raining. All it

---

ANGLER'S HINT

The best all-around outfit for backpacking is a four-section combination rod with both spinning and fly fishing capability. Pay special attention to protecting your rod with a rigid case.

---

does is hold the down in place, and that very gently.

Because this kind of jacket is so delicate, it is not popular in the United States. For sheer comfort, however, it is unparalleled. It is like living in a cloud of perfect temperature. For those who like it, it is well worth carrying a cheap plastic poncho for real downpours. While it is distinctly a minority opinion, one of the authors has used a jacket of this type for fifteen years, and it still has a few good years left in it.

Most American jackets are more sturdy, with outer shells designed to endure the knocks of trail traveling. There is still some difference in the weight of the outer shell between various makes, so keep an eye out not

---

BACKPACKER'S HINT

Backpacking comfort has more to do with your mental attitudes than with equipment. Most packers find their overall comfort is improved by planning carefully to carry only what they really need. The luxury is provided by nature—and you don't have to pack it in.

ANGLER'S HINT

Plan to fish at every opportunity along the trail. Your fishing begins as soon as you start. With pole and fishing vest handy, it only takes a few moments to try out a likely looking spot along the way.

only for durability but for sheer, sensual comfort. After all, the reason you are going backpacking in the first place is for pleasure. Make it as pleasurable as possible.

Another general principle to be observed in backpacking clothing, is *looseness*. Tight-fitting pants work against your leg muscles, and will fatigue you more quickly. The ever-present jeans are not the best choice for backpacking. They impede easy movement and good ventilation. The same is true of shirts, sweaters, and all other gear. Anything that restricts easy movement or adequate ventilation should be avoided.

PLANNING

Planning your backpacking trip is not only a necessity, it is one of the great pleasures. It extends the enjoyment of the venture by weeks, as you research where you are going, and how you will do it.

Unless you are already familiar with the area, good research is a necessity. Most of the areas in which you will backpack are regulated by some branch of government—the National Parks, Wilderness areas, Bureau of Land Management lands, etc. The agencies regulating public lands are acting in the *public* interest, at least in theory. Your primary sources of information will be those agencies, and the experience of other anglers who have been there.

Incidentally, the information you receive from any of these sources will depend somewhat on how specific your questions are. Very general inquiries will most likely be answered with general brochures.

There is also a difference in how "deep" you can go in any of the agencies—your aim in this research is to narrow down from a national or state agency to the most local branch you can find.

You assume that someplace on the local level there's an enthusiastic fly fisherman who is just dying to tell you what you want to know. Sometimes you never get past officialdom, but if you keep narrowing your focus, you will be surprised at how often you end up with a detailed personal letter with just the information you need.

In this kind of research it is more efficient to start with the general and narrow down to the specific. You will be surprised how far you can get with just a few phone calls.

In Chapter Eleven you will find a starting list of public agencies, the "broad picture," so to speak. Your research will be a several-step process, in which you narrow down from national to regional to state to local offices—always looking for that one individual. It's a lot like following the clues of a detective story.

CHAPTER 10

SOME GREAT LOCATIONS

Covering the good fishing locations in this country would extend to a whole series of books. In the scope of this book, we can mention only the highlights.

Since the primary quarry of the fly fisherman is some member of the trout family, we have limited our selection to trout waters.

The rivers and streams mentioned are some of the most popular trophy fish areas in the U.S. Even so, many excellent fishing grounds have been omitted. We've picked waters with an eye to the traveling angler, either on vacation or on business. These waters have historically provided good angling for the novice as well as the expert.

Some form of fly fishing is available to the angler year round. The peak season coincides with the "hatch" of various insect species, which varies with the individual stream. Generally speaking, spring to late summer can be considered the main season, but the angler should not overlook the possibilities of off-season fishing in his area.

PLANNING THE TRIP

When planning a trip in spring or early summer, try to pick an area with a choice of several streams. Give yourself as much time as possible, as early season fishing can be a hit-or-miss proposition. Spring runoffs and thaws are unpredictable, and a sudden flood can render an otherwise good stream quite hopeless. This unpredictability can last through June, particularly in Western drainages.

Contacting a local guide service or tackle shop can prevent a lot of frustration, particularly if your time is limited. And for most of us, limited time is the rule rather than the exception. The local tackle shop will be able to give you information on water levels, weather, major hatch periods, and general fishing conditions. Many also provide access maps of the local area, which are invaluable.

When fishing outside of your own area, be sure you have all the proper permits, and know the local regulations.

Many areas, in particular trophy trout streams, have specific regulations for different sections of the stream. You may find fly-only streams, barbless hooks, specified creel limits, or catch-and-release on different portions of the same stream.

Bear in mind the delicacy of our sport. The local regulations are designed to insure that we will be able to fish these streams ten years from now, and they should have every angler's whole-hearted support.

Proper planning and research is the major factor in a successful trip, particularly when away from your home area.

NORTHEASTERN U.S.

The heritage of American fly fishing began in the clear limestone streams of New England, and the northeastern U.S. is steeped in fly fishing history.

The first truly American fly patterns were created on these streams, and even today some of the most famous and creative fly tyers are in this area. Every angler owes it to himself to fish rivers like the Battenkill, Letort, or Beaverkill, for he will be casting a line into angling history.

The rivers of New England still hold trophy trout that will test the skill and patience of the most avid angler. Fishing these streams can be a truly emotional experience.

On these classic streams, you will find your best bet is classic patterns, as this is where they were developed.

Dry Patterns for the NE

1. Henderson
2. Quill Gordon
3. Iron Blue Dun
4. Ginger Quill

Nymphs

1. Mayfly
2. Caddis
3. Stonefly

Streamers

1. Black-Nosed Dace
2. Royal Coachman
3. Muddler Minnow

Terrestrials

1. Letort Cricket
2. Letort Hopper

Battenkill River, southwest Bennington County, Vermont. The Battenkill is one of the most famous trout rivers in North America. It contains medium-size brook trout, and large browns.

In the Manchester-Arlington Valley stretch the river is deep and slow-moving, with brushy banks. Below Arlington (along Route 313), the stream is tree-lined with a gravel bottom.

From Arlington there is good access into New York, which has a trophy trout section. Best fishing usually occurs in late May and early June, during the Hendrickson hatch.

From midsummer to fall, the major hatch is of the tiny Tricorythodes black-and-white (mayflies). You will probably want small hooks, size 24 and 26.

Fishing for the big browns in deeper holes, you can use big Muddlers and streamers.

Beware of the Battenkill, as it will test your skill. Many an experienced angler has gone home claiming there were no fish left in the river. They are there, but they don't catch themselves.

Letort Spring Run, south-central Cumberland County, Pennsylvania. The Letort, too, is one of the most fa-

---

ANGLER'S HINT

Enthusiastic hikers are not necessarily your best companions for a fishing trip. Fishermen are. Be sure you all have the same idea of what the trip is about.

---

mous limestone streams in American angling literature.

The Letort's big brown trout thrive in the cool, clear water, and they are *very* selective. Wading is not allowed, and fishing from the bank is most productive from a kneeling position.

In the summer months good patterns are the Letort Cricket and Letort Hopper. A variety of other terrestrials will sometimes work, as well as dries and small shrimp patterns.

There is good fishing from the quarry into Carlisle, Pennsylvania, and you will find many local access roads off Highway I-81.

Yellow Breeches, Cumberland County, Pennsylvania. Another well-known Cumberland County limestone creek. You'll find 38 miles of good fishing, with access from Carlisle along Routes 34 and 74. Yellow Breeches has excellent mayfly hatches. Again, tiny terrestrials (size 24 and 26) are also good.

Beaverkill River, southeast-central New York. The Beaverkill has a number of excellent public-access pools, such as the Junction Pool in Roscoe (where the Willowemoc and Beaverkill meet). Spring fishing is best.

The Beaverkill holds good brown trout and some rainbows. In the high spring waters, big Muddlers, streamers, nymphs and Stoneflies work well. There is good access off old Route 17, downstream from Roscoe.

There are a number of excellent fly tyers in the towns of Roscoe and Livingston Manor.

Big, Little Hunting Creek, Frederick County, Maryland. This is probably the best-known Maryland stream, containing rainbows and browns up to 18 inches. Much of the stream is restricted to fly fishing only.

Early spring fishing is good with streamers such as the Gray Ghost, as well as the ever present Muddlers. There is also a Green Drake hatch that normally occurs around the middle of May.

Good access from U.S. 15 at Thurmont, MD, and also from Route 77 West.

THE SOUTH

The South is best known for its warm-water fish, like bass. However, it does have one river that might even be your best bet in North America for a true trophy trout.

White River, north-central Arkansas. The White River holds trophy-size browns and rainbows. The largest brown on record is 33 pounds! The White provides some 80 miles of good fishing water, and a year-round 52-degree temperature makes it one of the richest rivers of its size in North America.

Fishing is good all year long, and can be excellent in May and June. During the warmer months, the cool of morning and late evening are most productive. Best patterns are Scuds, Sowbugs, Sculpin, Muddlers, and Crawfish.

Popular angling areas are off U.S. 62 from Mountain Home to Cotter, and Route 5 south from Mountain Home to Allison.

MIDWEST

The upper Midwest offers some of America's best trout fishing. Streams running into the Great Lakes hold not only the traditional browns, brookies, and rainbows but now contain runs of steelhead, chinook and coho salmon.

Steelhead, from 10 to 20 pounds, enter Great Lakes streams from mid-October through November. In more northerly areas, some fish will enter even later.

Standard steelhead patterns such as Skunks, Thors, Two-Egg Sperms, Wooly Worms, and Bright Marabous work well.

Most of these rivers have good hatches beginning in early spring. For browns and rainbows, you'll have good luck with Blue-Winged Olives, Hendricksons, and Sulfur Duns.

In June, you'll probably want Caddis and Yellow Stoneflies, Light Cahills, Pale Evening Duns and Brown/Gray/Yellow Drakes.

In late summer there is a large Michigan Caddis hatch, for which you'll want hooks in sizes 2 to 6.

Good patterns for brook trout in the upper Great Lakes areas are Adams, Royal Coachman, Humpies, Wulffs, and classic streamers such as Mickey Finn, Black-Nosed Dace, and Marabous.

Au Sable River, Lower Peninsula, Michigan. This is the state's best-known fly fishing area, and is a top producer of brownies and steelhead. The headwaters, above Grayling, are also excellent for brookies.

The Au Sable has a number of special regulations, depending on the section of the river being fished. You should check with local authorities and tackle shops first.

The best fishing on the Au Sable is early in the season. Morning and evening are the best times for the big browns that made Au Sable famous.

On dark days, a Blue-Winged Olive works well, as do big nymphs and streamers.

Access is from U.S. 23 at Oscoda (the river mouth). Also from Routes 33 and 72 at Mio, and roads north of Route 72 West, to Grayling.

Pere Marquette, Lower Peninsula, Michigan. This is small, classic trout water, and a top stream for brownies and steelhead. There are several branches to the stream, and a number of special regulations— check locally.

Fishing is good in the fall, with standard steelhead and trout patterns. The river also contains some Atlantic salmon.

Access is from U.S. 10, from Ludington east to Chase.

THE WEST

Western rivers are the mecca for fly fishermen. The sheer variety of Western waters is astonishing. You can fish everything from meadow streams to high Alpine lakes, from small spring creeks to big boiling rivers.

Western anglers need a veritable arsenal of flies to accommodate this wide range of conditions. Many rivers have had specific flies associated with them, such as the giant Stoneflies of the Madison, the tiny Mayflies of

Henry's Fork, and the Elk Hair Caddis of the Beaverhead.

In addition to these specialized flies, Marabou Muddlers, Sculpin, and giant nymphs are also highly productive. Once again, you will save a lot of time and frustration by consulting with local anglers and tackle shops.

Madison River, southwest Montana. The Madison is a big river with heavy water. Below Hebgen Lake, wading can be even dangerous. However, fishing for large browns and rainbows can be very rewarding.

Float trips arranged by a local guide are the best way to fish the 70-mile stretch from Quake Lake to Ennis.

The key fishing time on the Madison is from late June through July. There's an excellent salmon fly hatch in late June.

Try patterns such as a Sofa Pillow, Elk-Hair Salmon flies, Bitch Creek, Goddard Caddis, and Montana Stonefly.

Access to the Madison is from Route 287.

Yellowstone River, south-central Montana. Another big river, famous for cutthroat, rainbows, and browns. During the early season high water, floating is best. Later on, when the waters have lowered, wading is good.

Generally the best fishing is mid-July through August for dries, and September/October for streamers.

Key dry patterns for the Yellowstone are Elk-Hair Salmon Fly, Royal Wulff, Joe's Hopper, and Goddard Caddis. Good streamers are Spruce

Fly, Muddler, and Sculpins. Nymphs also fish well. Try Brown Stone and Hare's Ear.

Access is from U.S. 89, south from Livingston, Montana.

Big Hole River, southwest Montana. The Big Hole is an excellent early season river, with brookies and grayling in the upper stretches, as well as trophy browns and rainbows throughout.

Again, the high water of early spring makes raft fishing best, though the river is definitely wadable in late summer and early fall.

There is a good salmon fly hatch in early June. The most popular patterns locally are Salmon Fly, Humpies, Royal Wulff, Goddard Caddis, large Stonefly Nymphs, Brown Bear Black, Muddlers, and Sculpins.

The really prime fishing time on the Big Hole is June 15 to July 15. Access is along Route 43 at Divide, Wise River, and Wisdom. Southwest of Butte in the Melrose area, there is also access from U.S. 91 and I-15.

Beaverhead River, southwest Montana. This is a smaller river, with good-sized browns and rainbows. It's a tough river to wade, deep and brushy in many areas. The best method generally is floating. Many large fish are taken from under overhangs and deep undercut banks.

The best fishing month is usually July. Popular patterns are Troth Elk-Hair Caddis, Royal Wulff, Black Rubber Legs, Muddlers, Sculpin, Brown Bear Blacks, and Browns.

Access to the Beaverhead is along U.S. 41 north from Dillon, Montana.

Clark's Fork, western Montana. Clark's Fork is another excellent river for the early season. The headwaters are particularly good for cutthroat and brookies, while the lower section holds rainbows and browns.

Midges and mayflies produce well as early as April. There is a June salmon fly hatch, and July to August sees a series of caddis hatches.

Most popular patterns are Caddis Pupa, Joe's Hopper, Muddler Minnows, Salmon Flies, Adams, Humpies, and Stonefly Nymphs.

Access is from I-90 around Anaconda, Alder Lodge, and Missoula.

Armstrong and Nelson's Spring Creeks, south-central Montana. These are fee-fishing spring creeks in the Livingston, Montana area, and reservations are required. The quality of both fishing water and fish is superb, and the streams are easily wadable.

The best dry-fly fishing is in July, although it is very good year-round, for challenging browns and rainbows. Popular patterns: Light Olive Dun, Olive Drake Nymphs, Midges, and Light Olive Compara Dun.

Access is off I-90 to Livingston, Montana.

Henry's Fork (of the Snake), southeastern Idaho. Another large stream with good browns and rainbows. The two principal areas are the large box canyon below Island Park Dam, and the famous Railroad Ranch, which is meadow waters.

The canyon area is best fished with a drift boat through June, though it can be waded late in the season. The most popular patterns for the canyon are Stonefly Nymphs, Sofa Pillow, Royal Wulff, caddis patterns, and Light Olive Duns.

The Railroad Ranch area has a particularly good fly-fishing-only section. It is easily wadable, but the fish are extremely selective. Light leader and small flies are the norm here. Try Light Olive No-Hackle, Compara Duns, Green Drake, Elk-Hair Caddis, Poly-Wing Spinners, and Hoppers, all in small sizes.

Access is along U.S. 20-191 northeast from Idaho Falls, and southwest from West Yellowstone, Montana.

Silver Creek, south-central Idaho. This is a famous and fertile spring creek in the Sun Valley area, a meadow stream holding excellent rainbows. The river is wading only, with different regulations on the upper and lower stretches.

Silver Creek fishes best in late summer, when there is exceptionally rich insect life. Good patterns are Pale Mounding Dun, Yellow Spinner, Blue-Winged Olive, Hoppers, Brown Mayfly Nymph, Gray Drake Nymph, Renegade, and Royal Wulff.

Access is from U.S. 93 and U.S. 20, north of Twin Falls, Idaho.

THE NORTHWEST

Deschutes River, central Oregon. The Deschutes is a major Oregon steelhead and trout river. The upper reaches, around Bend, Oregon, are the state's best brown trout water. Below Bend is excellent rainbow fishing.

Above Bend, floating is your best bet, as the river is fast, and the bottom rocky and slippery. There is no fishing permitted from boats below Bend.

From the Warm Springs Indian Reservation to the Columbia River is fly and lure fishing only. This lower river is excellent summer steelhead fishing.

Trout fishing on the Deschutes is good from May through October, and the steelhead are good in September/October.

Popular trout patterns: Stonefly Nymphs, Hare's-Ear Nymphs, Wooly Worms, Muddlers, Elk-Hair Caddis, Tied Down Caddis.

Good steelhead patterns are small sizes of Skunk, Silver Hilton, Skykomish Sunrise, Fall Favorite, and Royal Coachman.

Access to the Deschutes is from U.S. 197 to U.S. 97, south from the Dalles through Maupin, Redmond, and Bend. Use local roads west to the river.

Umpqua River, southwest Oregon. This is a very popular river with a year-round steelhead season that peaks from November to February. Also good catches of rainbow, browns, brook, and sea-run cutthroat.

Above Rock Creek, the north fork has a fly-fishing-only stretch for steelhead and trout. The Umpqua is famous for summer steelhead (on flies) between Glade and Steamboat, from July through September.

Popular steelhead patterns are: Green-Butted Skunk, Black Rubber Leg Nymphs, Two-Egg Sperm, Skykomish Sunrise, and McCloud Ugly.

Trout patterns: Stonefly Nymphs, Hare's-Ear Nymphs, Muddlers, Royal Wulff, Humpies, Elk-Hair Caddis, Adams, and large streamers.

Access is along Routes 38 and 138, upriver from Reedsport to Roseburg:

then Routes 99 and 227 up the south fork, and Route 138 up the north fork.

Rogue River, southwest Oregon. The Rogue is considered a top western steelhead river, with the largest fish being taken between December and early spring. There is also excellent summer and early fall "half-pounder" fishing, a real treat for the fly fisherman. The upper valley holds rainbows, brooks, browns, and cutthroats.

The Rogue, like many western rivers, has limited access for waders, and floating the canyon is the best method.

Favorite local patterns: Rogue River Special, Golden Demon, Red and Silver Ants, Royal Coachman Bucktail, and Maverick.

Access roads to lower river downstream from Grants Pass. Above Grants Pass, access is from Routes 227 and 62.

Skagit River, northwest Washington. Many steelhead in the 20-pound class are taken from the Skagit. Winter runs go from February through March, with summer runs continuing through September.

The Skagit also sees large runs of spring/fall salmon, summer/fall sea-run cutthroat, and Dolly Varden.

The Skagit is another fast and deep river. It can be fished from the bank, but floating is more versatile.

Steelhead patterns: Fall Favorite, Golden Demon, Silver Hilton, Skunk, and McCloud Ugly.

Cutthroat patterns: Thor, Dead Chicken, Omnibus, Bucktail Coachman.

Access: North from Seattle on I-5

to Route 20 West. There is good access to the river all along Route 20.

Skykomish River, west-central Washington. This is a famous winter steelhead river, which peaks in December and January. Summer run steelhead come in June and July.

There is also a good coho salmon run in September/October, and cutthroat and Dolly Varden in summer and fall, making the Skykomish one of the most versatile of all Northwest rivers.

Float fishing is best, though many sections are wadable. The best fishing is found above the falls at Index, Washington.

Patterns: Skykomish Sunrise, Polar Shrimp, Fall Favorite, Silver Hilton, and Skunk.

Access: I-5 north from Seattle, exit on Route 2, which follows the river. Good access.

Kalama River, southwest Washington. The Kalama is very good for both winter and summer steelhead and sea-run cutthroat. July and August are the best months for summer steelhead on flies. The upper river is restricted to fly fishing only.

Patterns: Kalama Special, Skunk, Black Marabou, and Washougal Olive.

Access off I-5 north of Portland, Oregon. The road parallels the north bank of the Kalama.

Hoh River, Olympic Peninsula, Washington. The Hoh is a relatively large river that can be fished either from a boat or waded. The river remains clear in winter, unlike many Northwest streams, and there is an excellent winter steelhead run from December through February. The summer steelhead run lasts from May through October. In addition, there is a late-summer to fall run of sea-run cutthroat.

Patterns: Fall Favorite, Skykomish Sunrise, Single Egg, Skunk, Silver Hilton, and a variety of Marabous.

Access: U.S. 101 north from Aberdeen, Washington, to lower river, 20 mile road from 101 to upper river. Check locally.

CALIFORNIA

Fall River, north-central California. A fertile spring creek with good fly fishing for big rainbows and browns. Good mayfly and caddis hatches in May and early June.

Patterns: Olive Nymphs, Brown-Olive Spinners, Pale Morning Duns, Orange Caddis, and Yellow Stoneflies.

Access: Public access is difficult above Tule River except by boat, which has to be launched from Pacific Gas and Electric land. There is some public access off Route 299, northeast from Redding, California, to Fall River Mills and McArthur.

Hat Creek, northern California. One of California's best trout streams, holding trophy-size browns and rainbows. Good hatches of big Stoneflies in May and June.

Patterns: Yellow Humpies, Sofa Pillow, Green Drakes, Pale Morning Duns, Olive Caddis, and Yellow Caddis.

Access: There is good access from Route 89 in Lassen Park. Pacific Gas and Electric lands are open to the public.

CHAPTER 11

RESOURCES

There is a wide variety of fly fishing literature. It has even been seriously claimed that more words have been written about fly fishing than any other subject except the Bible. Rather than a long (and comparatively meaningless) bibliography, we have included here a small selection of publications of particular value.

BOOKS

Joe Brooks was one of the master outdoor writers of this century. Whatever his subject, he wrote with clarity and authority, and his books are highly recommended. With the exception of *Trout Fishing*, most of Brooks's books are now out of print, but may be found in some used book stores. As a general introduction to the subject, these two are particularly recommended:

Brooks, Joe. *Trout Fishing*. New York: Outdoor Life/Harper & Row, 1972.

Brooks, Joe. *Complete Book of Fly Fishing*. New York: Outdoor Life/ A. S. Barnes, 1968.

Doug Swisher and Carl Richards have written two books of considerable value to the fly fisherman, particularly the advanced angler. They are meticulous in detail, though not as general as Brooks's books. Particularly with respect to perfect imitation of natural insects, Swisher and Richards are excellent. For the advanced fly fisherman, these can be considered essential.

Swisher, Doug, and Richards, Carl. *Selective Trout.* **New York: Crown Publishers, 1971.**
Swisher, Doug, and Richards, Carl. *Fly Fishing Strategy.* **New York: Crown Publishers, 1975.**

Special mention should be made of Ernie Schwiebert's monumental two-volume work on trout. This is probably the most comprehensive treatment ever given a sport fish, and stands as a monument to Schwiebert's scholarship, experience, and understanding.

Schwiebert, Ernie. *Trout.* **New York: E. P. Dutton, 1976.**

A. J. McClane was long the fishing editor of *Field and Stream.* He wrote *The Practical Fly Fisherman* thirty years ago, just as the technological revolution of Fiberglas and graphite was beginning to have an impact on the sport. However, his comments on basic technique and his innate fish sense make him well worth reading today.

McClane, A. J. *The Practical Fly Fisherman.* **Englewood Cliffs, N.J.: Prentice-Hall, 1953.**

McClane was also the general editor of what is still the best overall encyclopedia of fishing lore. While it is not exclusively about fly fishing, there is a wealth of information on that as well as all other kinds of fishing. This is recommended for every fisherman's library.

McClane, A. J., ed. *McClane's Standard Fishing Encyclopedia.* **New York: Holt, Rinehart and Winston, 1974.**

Another useful encyclopedia has much broader coverage, dealing with hunting, game animals, camping, and archery, as well as fishing. Not as essential for the fisherman as the McClane encyclopedia, but a useful and interesting addition.

Sparano, Vin T. *Complete Outdoors Encyclopedia.* **New York: Outdoor Life/Harper & Row, 1973.**

Perhaps the most spectacularly illustrated book is a recent publication of the Golden Press, a part of their Hunting and Fishing Library. In full-color throughout, some of the photographs of fish approaching and taking bait are unequalled. Here again, fly fishing is only a part of the coverage, but the book is worth having, if only for the underwater photography.

Sternberg, Dick. *The Art of Freshwater Fishing.* **New York: The Golden Press, 1982.**

Lefty Kreh has authored (or co-authored) several books of value to the fly fisherman. He was one of the original founding members of the Salt Water Fly Rodder's Association.

Kreh, Lefty (Bernard). *Fly Fishing in Salt Water.* **New York: Crown Publishers, 1974.**
Kreh, Lefty (Bernard) and Sosin, Mark. *Practical Fishing Knots.* **New York: Crown Publishers, 1972.**

There is a very unusual book by Gary Borger, a fisherman/botany professor, which is virtually a complete text on streamside entomology. For the fly fisherman who becomes involved (obsessed may be a better word) with exact matching of his fly to the natural food, this book is the ultimate. Borger deals with the life cycles and forms of all the common aquatic insects, and gives detailed directions for tying flies to match them. Excellent illustrations by Robert Pils.

Borger, Gary. *Naturals: A Guide to Food Organisms of the Trout.* Harrisburg, Pa.: Stackpole Books, 1980.

If the possibilities of combining fishing with backpacking appeal to you, there is a book devoted entirely to that subject.

Farmer, Charles. *Backpack Fishing.* Paramus, N.J.: Jolex, Inc., 1976.

There are a number of books available on the art of fly tying. Most of them are useful and good—it isn't really possible to choose a "best." However, this book is a good beginning, taking you step by step through the basic fly designs for dries, wets, streamers, and nymphs.

Bay, Kenneth. *How to Tie Freshwater Flies.* Tulsa, Okla.: Winchester Press, 1970.

In the Western U.S., there is a somewhat different style of fly tying, accommodating the differences in Eastern and Western fishing. For an introduction to the Western style:

Dennis, Jack, Jr. *Western Trout Fly Tying Manual*, 2 vols. Jackson Hole, Wyoming: Snake River Books, 1974.

On the more anecdotal side, artist/angler Russell Chatham has edited *Silent Seasons*, an anthology of excellent literary quality, containing twenty-one fishing adventures by seven American experts, some of whom write as well as they fish. Chatham's other book, *The Angler's Coast*, is made up of his own reflections on waters and fishermen he has known over the years.

Chatham, Russell, ed. *Silent Seasons.* New York: E. P. Dutton, 1978.
Chatham, Russell. *The Angler's Coast.* New York: Doubleday & Co., 1976.

There is an extremely funny, moving, and powerful new novel whose principal character is a fly fisherman. Gus, the protagonist of *The River Why*, was born of a world-famous purist fly fisherman, and a backwoods Oregon woman perfectly content to beat a fish about the head with her pole, if that was what it required. His life (and the book) revolves around his fishing adventures and escapades. You won't get much technical information out of this, but it may show you some aspects of fly fishing you've never dreamed of.

Duncan, David James. *The River Why.* San Francisco: Sierra Club Books, 1983.

MAGAZINES

The general outdoor magazines are listed here because they frequently publish articles on fly fishing in specific areas, and some have columns devoted to the sport.

Back issues of these magazines are a treasure trove of information on fly fishing. You can consult the *Reader's Guide to Periodical Literature* at your local library to find specific articles that are of interest to you in back numbers.

In addition to the general outdoor magazines, several magazines deal only with fly fishing. *The Flyfisher* is the official publication of the Federation of Fly Fishermen, and *Trout* is the membership publication of Trout Unlimited.

Outdoor Life. 380 Madison Ave., New York, NY 10017

Sports Afield. 250 West 55th Street, New York, NY 10019

Field and Stream. 1515 Broadway, New York, NY 10036

Fly Fisherman Magazine. Ziff-Davis Publishing Co., Dorset, VT 05251

The Flyfisher. 390 Bella Vista, San Francisco, CA 94127

Trout. P.O. Box 992, Taunton, MA 02780

The Fly Tyer. 1231 Rt. 16, North Conway, NH 03860

CATALOGS

The catalogs of tackle manufacturers and outdoor outfitters are a valuable source of information. Not only will they tell you what is available in the way of equipment, but many of them have valuable hints on fishing practice, fly selection, and so forth. Some manufacturers also publish pamphlets on various subjects related to fly fishing. When you write for their catalogs, ask if any such publications are available.

Those included here give a good perspective on the peripheral gear of fly fishing, such as clothing, camping equipment, etc.

Dan Bailey Flies & Tackle. P.O. Box 1019, Livingston, MT 59047

Orvis. Manchester, VT 05254

Kaufmann's Streamborn. P.O. Box 23032, Portland, OR 97223

Scientific Anglers. P.O. Box 33984, St. Paul, MN 55144

Eddie Bauer, Inc. P.O. Box 3700, Seattle, WA 98124

L. L. Bean. Freeport, ME 04033

Cortland Line Company. Cortland, NY 13045

Fenwick. Box 729, Westminster, CA 92683

The Garcia Corporation. 329 Alfred Ave., Teaneck, NJ 07666

Sage. 9630 LaFayette St., Bainbridge Island, WA 98110

Scientific Anglers, a manufacturer of fly lines, has published a series of small booklets you would find useful.

"Fly Fishing for Panfish"
"The Fly Fishing Handbook"
"Fly Fishing Made Easy"
"Fly Rodding for Bass"
"Saltwater Fly Fishing"

ORGANIZATIONS

The organizations listed here are national in scope. Some have local chapters all over the country. The national organization will be able to provide you with the address of the chapter in your area.

Trout Unlimited. P.O. Box 992, Taunton, MA 02780

Theodore Gordon Fly Fishers. 24 E 39th St., New York, NY

Federation of Fly Fishers. P.O. Box 1088, West Yellowstone, MT 59758

International Game Fish Association (world records). 3000 East Las Olas Blvd., Fort Lauderdale, FL 33316

GOVERNMENT SOURCES

Bureau of Sport Fisheries and Wildlife: Department of the Interior, Washington, DC 20240. This is a good source of general information about fishing on public lands. When you write for information, be sure to request a listing of their regional offices, which will be able to give you more specific information about local areas.

State Fish and Game Depts: Every state has some such agency, which you can find in the telephone book under State Government. The main office will be located either in the state capital, or in the state's largest city. If you write to the Information and Education Division, your letter will usually be routed to the right place (even if your local department doesn't have such a division).

This is probably your best source of detailed information on prospec-

tive back country fishing. A fisheries division, if listed, is also a good source.

The U.S. Forest Service: Department of Agriculture, Washington, DC 20250. The national office will probably not be of much assistance except to give you a list of regional offices. If you can locate the regional office (again, the phone book is your best source), you can probably skip the national office.

From the regional offices you can get a list of the forests each administers, and the ranger in charge. Write directly to the forest ranger in charge of the forest, with a very specific letter.

Whether you're querying by phone or mail, always ask for recommendations of people on the local level you might talk to. One of the best ways of threading your way through any bureaucracy is by asking for *names of individuals* who might know what you're looking for.

This technique works very well with the Forest Service, and it usually isn't long before you're in touch with a fellow outdoorsman. But you do have to get to the field offices, not the bureaucratic ones.

National Park Service: Interior Building, Washington, DC 20240. You can save a step here by going directly to one of the regional offices: the Northeast Regional office is in Philadelphia, Southeast in Richmond, VA, Midwest in Omaha, Southwest in Santa Fe, Western in San Francisco, and Northwest in Seattle. Telephone information will give you current numbers.

Bureau of Land Management: Department of the Interior, Washington, DC 20240. BLM administers an enormous amount of public land, particularly in the West. Good maps are available from them, and sometimes good information.

Of these agencies, the State Fish and Game Departments, and the Forest Service are the best bets.

INFORMATION AND EQUIPMENT SOURCES

NORTHEAST
L. L. Bean, Inc.
Freeport, ME 04033
207-865-3111
Orvis
Manchester, VT 05254
802-362-1300
Yellow Breeches Shoppe
Allenberry Road
Boiling Springs, PA 17007
717-258-6752
Eddie Bauer, Inc.
510 Boylston Street
Boston, MA 02116
617-262-6700
The Hatch
De Bruce Road
Livingston Manor, NY 12758
914-439-4944

SOUTH
Hunter Bradlee Co.
291 The Quadrangle
4025 N.W. Parkway
Dallas, TX 75203
214-744-1030
Orvis Houston
5848 Westheimer Road
Houston, TX 77057
713-783-2111

Dale Fulton
Fulton Fishing Service
Rt. 1, Box 176A
Cotter, AR 72626
501-430-5338

MIDWEST
Eddie Bauer, Inc.
123 North Wabash
Chicago, IL 60602
312-263-6005
Eddie Bauer, Inc.
821 Marquette Avenue
Minneapolis, MN 55402
612-339-9477
Eddie Bauer, Inc.
21110 Greenfield Road
Oak Park, MI 48237
313-967-0155
Gates Au Sable Lodge
Box 2828, R.R. 2
Grayling, MI 49738
517-348-8462

WEST
Dan Bailey's Flies & Tackle
209 West Park Street
P.O. Box 1019
Livingston, MT 59047
406-222-1673
Bob Jacklin's Fly Shop
Box 604
West Yellowstone, MT 59768
406-646-7336
Eddie Bauer, Inc.
220 Post Street
San Francisco, CA 94108
415-986-7600
Orvis San Francisco
166 Maiden Lane
San Francisco, CA 94108
415-392-1600

Al Troth
Box 1307
Dillon, MT 59725
406-683-2752
The Snug Co.
P.O. Box 598
Sun Valley, ID 83353
208-622-9305
Eddie Bauer, Inc.
1330 Fifth Avenue
Seattle, WA 98101
206-622-2766

INDEX

About Cam Sigler and Don Berry

A Cajun, born in southern Louisiana, Cam Sigler began fishing in the swamps and bayous at the age of five. His father worked on hydroelectric power projects, seldom staying in one place more than two years, and so Cam moved with his family throughout the South, fishing from project to project.

While still in his teens, Cam had the good fortune to meet world-famous author and fisherman Joe Brooks. Under his tutelage, Cam developed his skills as a fly caster with a special talent for catching big fish on lightweight tackle.

Following attendance at William and Mary College in Virginia and service in the Coast Guard, Cam's passion for fishing drew him to southern Florida. During the evening he worked as a bellhop, clocking out at midnight. By 8 A.M. he was in his boat at the marina, waiting to take the overflow of tourists needing a boat and a guide for the day's fishing. If nobody showed up by 9 A.M., he went fishing anyway.

In 1968, Cam moved west to manage the Eddie Bauer store in Seattle. An inducement, undoubtedly, was the Northwest's reputation for excellent fly fishing in rivers, lakes, and salt water.

Today, as the manager of the Eddie Bauer Commercial/International Sales operation, Cam travels the world to meet the demand for his company's line of outdoor clothing and equipment. Cam and his fly rods have taken fish from Alaska to the Gulf of Mexico, from the Atlantic to the Pacific, and points in-between. He's a celebrity in Japan, where he is heralded for his fishing expertise, and has been featured in that country's outdoor magazines.

A decorative wading staff, high on the wall of Cam's office, is a tribute to his sportsmanship and fishing skills from the Axolotl Society—a national group of outdoorsmen dedicated to the betterment of fly fishing. Cam's fellow members include bankers, professional athletes, stage and movie personalities, and even several United States astronauts for true diversity.

Don Berry is a prolific writer based in the Pacific Northwest. With eight books to his credit, he spends more time fishing for the right word than for brown trout, although he enjoys taking to the streams whenever he can.